New Second Music Reader ...

Luther Whiting Mason

THE NEW

SECOND MUSIC READER

BASED LARGELY UPON C. H. HOHMANN

GIVING FIRST LESSONS IN

READING MUSIC AT SIGHT

WITH ONE AND TWO-PART EXERCISES AND SONGS, AND
DIRECTIONS TO TEACHERS

BY

LUTHER WHITING MASON

BOSTON, U.S.A.:
PUBLISHED BY GINN & COMPANY.
1897.

Copyright, 1886, by LUTHER WHITING MASON

Typography of J. F. LOUGHLIN, 20 Hawley St., Boston.

PRESSWORK BY GINN & CO., BOSTON, U.S.A.

PREFACE.

THE prevalent desire for novelties has led many friends of this Method to deprecate the retention, in these revisions, of so many of the selections used in the first editions of the NATIONAL MUSIC COURSE; but while the author appreciates the full force of the popular taste, he also realizes the innate educational value of this material, which has become all the greater for its proven fitness. So much is this the fact, that after diligent search throughout Europe, especially in those centres where school music receives the fostering care of the state and the service of the best intellects, he has found it impossible to replace these selections, except in a few instances, inasmuch as they are important members of a carefully considered and well organized system, the rejection of which would materially injure the completeness of the whole.

There will be found, however, in the elaboration of the elementary portion of this book, much that is new and helpful to both teacher and pupil, the use of which has been made practicable by the general advancement of the science of teaching music in the schools — amongst which may be mentioned, Rhythmic Analyses (by means of Time-Names, as originally invented by the Author of this work); Preparatory Exercises in the Study of Two-Part Singing; German Chromatic Pitch-Names, adapted to American usage; Special Exercises in Singing Chromatic Sounds; Diagrams of the Scale in the Various Keys; and Going from One Key to Another, — together with suggestions to the teacher, at such points as seem to require particular treatment.

In the Introduction will be found interesting chapters on Tune and Time; Illustrative Preparatory Lessons for the use of such schools as commence this course with the NEW SECOND SERIES OF CHARTS and this READER.

Part IV contains Test-Exercises for individual reading, — which is seldom provided for, but which is as necessary in the study of music as in that of language, — to inspire the pupil with self-reliance.

In the Appendix is a full explanation of the system and use of Time-Names, the object of which is to designate the position of each note in a measure of whatever kind of time. This system does not pretend to teach or develop time, but simply to *name* the notes in any given measure. It differs entirely from the Chevé system of Time-Names (which has been adopted in the Tonic-Sol-Fa method in a modified form), as, in this system, the *measure* is the unit, while in the Chevé system the unit is a "*pulse*" or beat.

The New Second Series of National Music Charts are intended to accompany this Reader, and have received similar treatment in their preparation; and both should be used in connection, to secure the best results.

Finally, we will, in this as in former editions, call the teacher's attention to the following general directions :—

1. Require a good position of the pupils while singing.
2. Do not allow them to sing too *loud*, or to shout instead of singing.
3. Do not let them heavily *drag* the rhythm.
4. Do not permit coarseness of utterance or indistinct articulation.
5. From the very first, aim at imparting a generally soft style of singing as the basis of all expression.
6. Encourage liveliness and cordiality of manner, to preserve the buoyancy of the music.

Acknowledgments are due to Mrs. ADELIA L. LOUGHLIN, of Hyde Park, Mass., for translations (designated by a +); and to Mr. G. A. VEAZIE, Jr., of Chelsea, Mass., and others, for valuable assistance.

L. W. M.

BOSTON, April, 1886.

CONTENTS.

vi CONTENTS.

INTRODUCTION

TO THE

NEW SECOND NATIONAL MUSIC READER

"Multum in Parvo."

INTRODUCTION.

I.—TUNE.

THE object of this Introduction is to aid such teachers of common schools as know but little about music to teach a class of children from eight to eleven or twelve years of age to sing through the following course. It is very natural to suppose that, as this is the Second Reader, corresponding with the Second Series of Charts, it is necessary to have gone through the First. But it is not so. The First Reader and Charts are designed for children from five to eight years of age, and are not adapted to interest children beyond that age.

We have therefore prepared this Introduction to the Second, to be used *instead* of the First, Series of Music Charts and First Music Reader, for children the majority of whom are over eight years of age.

We would suggest as a course in rote-singing,—

(1.) The following songs from the Second Reader (only the melody of each):

"The Night is Gone," page 21.   "Evening Song,"   page   61.
"Awaking Song,"   "   34.   "Song of Praise,"   "   124.
"Morning Awaketh,"   "   35.   "The Bee's Lesson," "   126.
"Praise of Singing,"   "   54.

(2.) THE SCALE.—The teacher having written the diagram shown on page xviii of this book upon the blackboard, the scale is to be learned by rote *as a tune*, and is not to be explained nor talked about at present. It should be sung both by the numerals, or scale-names, and by the syllables, ascending and descending.

In every school where there has been no regular instruction in singing, the teacher may expect to find three classes:

1. The positively musical.
2. The passively musical.
3. The negatively musical.

The positively musical are those who have been accustomed to sing at home, in school, or in Sunday-school, so that they can sing several songs by rote, and are glad of the opportunity to learn more in this way.

The passive class are those who have sufficient musical talent, but it has never been called into exercise.

The negative, are those who have a talent for music, but have been led to believe they had not, by hearing it said that "there was no music in the families" to which they belong; and their parents and friends oppose music in schools, saying it is a waste of time and money, and an injustice to those who cannot learn to sing, etc.

The proportion of the positive class to the other two will depend upon the influences, musical, that have been brought to bear upon them up to the ages of eight or nine years. If the children have been accustomed to hear singing at home, at school, and in Sunday-school, and have not been discouraged by their parents and friends in their first attempts, there will be but very few of the negative class.

In commencing, let the teacher direct her attention to the positive class. *Do not urge* those who have not been accustomed to singing to join in the exercises at first. If any in their first attempts sing *out of tune,* the teacher should ask them to listen; but do not discourage them. Give them to understand that this is one way to learn to sing,—that is, *to listen.*

By way of encouragment, let the teacher establish some test of improvement. Our test is the scale. Let the teacher find out: How many can sing the scale alone; How many can sing up and down three sounds of the scale correctly; How many five or six sounds; and encourage those who are disposed to try, by telling them that if they can learn to sing the scale up and down correctly, they can learn to read music.

"Veazie's Music Primer," which is published by Messrs. Ginn & Co., will be found valuable at this stage of work, as it contains a carefully prepared set of progressive scale-exercises in figures, easy of comprehension, and admirably calculated to lead the pupil on toward the study of staff notation. Full directions are given in the work for the teacher's guidance; and as it quite inexpensive, there is no reason why any teacher should be without its aid.

II.—TIME.

Have you ever observed children following a band of Music,—how with lengthened strides they will endeavor to keep step to the measured strains of the march? or the boy with his clappers, giving out in smart, clear clicks the well-defined rhythm of some popular song,—this without any knowledge of music as a science, and only exhibiting a latent sense of that rhythm which is in and through all Nature?

If a boy marches well, keeping step to the music, or plays his clappers with more or less rhythmical accuracy, we say that the child keeps "good time," or is a good timist.

Now this sense of Time, like that of Tune, is not equally possessed by all children at first. To some it is just as natural to sing or play in time as it is to breathe; to others it is a matter of development; and to say that a child who does not at once show the ability is therefore incapable of attaining its possession, is unjust.

We give our school-children a fair trial in regard to tune, and with abundant success; let us be as fair in the matter of time.

We require precision in pitch when singing the sounds of the scale. We must be just as particular to require precision in time, in order to insure success in reading music at sight.

Precision of movement shall be the text of this chapter; and this should be the teacher's aim in her efforts to awaken "Time, in her classes,— trusting to the influence of the models of song presented in the course of study to round off all the sharp angles and finally produce a liberty of movement which shall never degenerate into license, but which shall always be pure, free, and graceful, and under the firm control of an educated will.

Although there is a wide difference of opinion among our native singing-teachers relative to the matter of teaching time, it is nevertheless true, that the surest and best results have followed in the train of those teachers of the past and present age who have faithfully and persistently held to the so-called "old fashioned" mode of *beating time with the hand.**

---

* Dr. JOHN HULLAH, Inspector of Music, in his Report on the Examination in Music of the Stu. dents of Training Schools in Great Britain for the year 1872, says: "If I were to point out any single shortcoming which in the course of these examinations has struck me more frequently

Wherever this method has been been loyally tried, it has worked successfully; and where it has proved unsuccessful, its failure may be fairly attributed to want of care and lack of persistent effort in its teaching. Beating time is in itself alone an art which requires as careful a training to master as do any of the beautiful calisthenic exercises which are the grace and pride of many a school-room; and it should for a time be classed as a special study, and a few minutes daily devoted to careful drill in its positions and movements.

The following directions may serve to assist the teacher in commencing the study of "Beating Time" as an Art. It must be remembered, however, that from the very first attempts the class must be carefully scrutinized, all laggards spurred up to work briskly, and kind encouragement given to those who are willing, but awkward, in their trials. After one series of classes have acquired the art, it will be very easy to keep it up.

THE ART OF BEATING TIME WITH THE HAND.

It is supposed that the sense of time has been developed to some degree, unconsciously, by means of rote-singing. The pupils are now to acquire the art of reading music from the notes; and this includes the ability to give each note in a measure its right length, as well as the right pitch, and that without any aid from the teacher.

The experience of centuries teaches that the best way to do this in singing is by some method of beating time with the hand. History also shows that all substitutes for this — such as metronomes, improvised pendulums, pinching one's self,* etc. — are failures so far as they tend to develop the ability to read music independently as to time.

POSITION FOR BEATING TIME.

Sit or stand erect, poising forward a little, with active chest. Place the elbows at the side, just far enough back to allow the middle finger of the right hand to touch the centre of the palm of the left.

---

than any other, it would not be in what is called 'a feeling' for *tune* but for *time.* I attribute this in a great measure to the insufficient attention given to 'beating time' with the hand. The indisposition of students to do this, and their clumsiness in doing it, are the best tributes to its usefulness."

*There is a method now before the public which recommends the pupils' pinching themselves, that they may "feel the time all through them." Such is the straining for "new departures"! To suppose that a thing must always be new to be good, is about as shallow as to take everything to be good because it is new. Let us hold fast to the good that we have till we have *proved* something new to be better.

The Downward and the Upward motions should be from the wrist only. This is very important, as it will not tire the pupils so soon, and they will be less liable to jerk the body while beating. Some children will require special instruction and drill in this, as they will not be able at first to make much motion from the wrist. A good plan, perhaps, is to direct the pupils to seize the right wrist with the left hand in a firm grip, and then to move the right hand up and down, like a pigeon's wing in flying. The teacher can do this while the pupils imitate her, and most of them will get a clear idea of the motion from the wrist.

The teacher may now proceed somewhat as follows: —

LESSON I.

BEATING TWO-PART MEASURE.— POSITION.

Teacher. Attention!

[The pupils give their attention.]

T. Place your hands as I do mine!

[*a.* The teacher places her hands so that the end of the middle finger of the right hand shall rest in the centre of the palm of the left, and draws the elbows well back, bringing the forearms into a horizontal position, quite close to the body. The pupils imitate her with more or less success at first, but finally all do it very well; for it is not very difficult.]

T. You are doing very well indeed. Now watch me, and do as I do!

[*b.* The teacher raises her hand from its horizontal position to a nearly upright one, by a quick motion from the wrist only, and keeps her hand in that position. The pupils imitate her.]

T. [*With her hand still in upright position.*] When I say, Position for beating time, I wish you to place your hands as you have them now. Watch me again, and do as I do. Attention!

[Teacher drops her hands at her sides. The class imitates her.]

T. Very well. Position for beating time!

[Many of the pupils understand, and take the position promptly; some move indolently, others place the left hand above the right. and so on.]

T. Some of you did quite well. But I want you all to do it well; and to do that, you must be smart, quick, about it.

When I say, Attention, drop your hands at your sides. Attention!

[Teacher drops hands at her sides. The pupils imitate her.]

T. Position for beating time!

[Teacher again takes position, as at *b*, and the pupils imitate her more successfully, as a class, than at first. As this is the first step, it will be better to be quite sure of it before proceeding farther; and it may need several trials to enable all to take the position promptly.]

LESSON II.

TWO—PART MEASURE CONTINUED.— BEATING.

Teacher. Attention!

[Teacher and pupils drop their hands at their sides.]

T. Watch me, now, and notice what I do.

[Teacher places her hands in position for beating time; then, bringing the right hand down into the position described at *a*, asks,—]

T. Which way did my hand go then?
Pupils. It went down.
T. Yes; and we will call it the Downward Beat, and this [*raising the right hand to position* b,] the Upward Beat; and the two beats we will call a *measure.* Now watch me, and tell me how many measures I beat:

*Down*ward beat, upward beat *Down*ward beat, upward beat.
P. Two measures.
T. Very good. Now you may try. Position for beating time !

[Pupils take position.]

T. Beat two measures.

------

* In these lessons the teacher will say nothing about accent; but will be careful to give an emphasis to the syllable or word *Down*, in naming the down beat, in all measures, and a slight stress to the word *Right*, in naming that beat in four-part measure, and be careful that the class imitate her in this respect. This is better than talking too much about accent at first.

[The teacher and class beat two measures, naming the beats, and then four; and continue until a fair degree of uniformity and precision of movement is established.]

In nearly all classes there will be found some pupils who are inclined to keep the hand in constant *aimless* motion. Such require particular attention, and should be led to observe that after each beat the hand remains perfectly quiet; also, that the motions should be quick and decisive, but without noise from the hands.

At this stage, if desirable, the lessons in singing from figures can be taken up, and carried as far as Exercise 25.

LESSON III.

BEATING THREE-PART MEASURE.

T. Attention! You will notice again what I do.

[Teacher places her hands in position for beating time, and gives the down-beat, saying *Down;* then moves the right hand smartly to the left, so that the base of the thumb shall touch the body, saying *Left;* and from that upward to the first position, saying *Up;* — these three movements being done with steadiness, and with a studied angularity, that each motion may be perfectly clear to the pupils.]

T. How many beats did I make then?
P. Three.
T. What did I call them?
P. Down, Left, Up.
T. Good! That is called Beating three-part measure. Watch me, and tell me how many three-part measures I beat: [*beating*] *Down,* Left, Up; *Down,* Left, Up; *Down,* Left, Up; *Down,* Left, Up.
P. Four measures.
T. Very well. You may try: Position for beating time! Beat two measures of three-part time, naming the beats.

[Pupils try, but find it more difficult than beating two-part measure. The teacher patiently encourages, until a fair degree of proficiency is attained; when Exercises in Figures from No. 26 to No. 36 may be taught.

LESSON IV.

BEATING FOUR—PART MEASURE.

T. Attention! Watch me again, and notice what I do.

[Teacher places her hands in position, and gives the down- and left-beats, naming them; then says *Right,* moving the *right* hand from the body, the fingers sweeping over the palm and resting upon the fingers of the left hand*; then from that to the first position, saying *Up.*]

T. How many beats did I make?
P. Four.
T. What did I call them?
P. Down, Left, Right, Up.
T. Yes. That is called four-part measure. Look again, and tell me how many four-part measures I beat: [*beating*] Down, Left, *Right,* Up; Down, Left, *Right,* Up.
P. Two measures.
T. Very good. Now you may try: Position for beating time! Beat one measure. Beat two measures. Beat four measures.

[There will be found little difficulty with this kind of measure if two-part and three-part have been thoroughly taught. The Exercises in Figures may now be concluded.

---

* In the beating of four-part measure, the attention of the teacher is called particularly to the position of the *right hand* after the performance of the right-beat;—its fingers resting upon those of the left (and not on the palm, as after the down-beat). It is essential that this position be carefully explained to the scholars, as it will be of great value to them hereafter in the practice of Time-Names.

TIME-NAMES. Time-names should not be used in connection with the first practice of the art of beating time, but should only be taught in connection with the study of staff-notation; and not then, until the sense of tune and time has a certain degree of development. They will then be found a most valuable auxiliary in the study of singing at sight, provided they are used always with the beating of the time by the hand. A keener sense of rhythm will thus be established in the mind of the pupil, especially as regards the minute subdivisions of measure, enabling him finally to grasp with ease and confidence the *Motives, Sections,* and even *Phrases* of his exercises and songs.

ILLUSTRATIVE LESSONS

PREPARATORY TO THE NEW SECOND SERIES MUSIC CHARTS, AND
NEW SECOND MUSIC READER.

For pupils from eight to ten or eleven years of age.

LESSON I.

Teacher. Many of you can sing several songs which you have learned by *rote,* or by hearing other people till you were able to join in singing them; and it will be very pleasant for you to learn more songs in that way. You are now old enough to take pleasure in learning to read music, as you can now read words which you at first learned to speak by hearing other people talk, or by *rote.* If you are very attentive, and all who can sing will do the best they can, you will make rapid progress.

All listen to me!

[Teacher sings.]

La, la, la, la, la, la, la, la.

T. All may sing as I did.

[Eight or ten of the class sing correctly, *and the teacher should be very careful to let the whole class share the credit.*]

T. That is very well. I will sing again, and you notice in which direction my voice seems to go in passing from one sound to another.

[Teacher sings the ascending scale.]

Pupils. Your voice went up as by steps.

T. That is a very good answer. Listen again, and notice which way my voice goes.

[Teacher sings the descending scale.]

P. Your voice went down.

T. Yes. I will sing upwards, as I did at first, and you count the number of sounds I sing one above the other.

[Teacher sings the ascending scale.]

P. Eight.

T. You may sing eight sounds, as I did.

[A large proportion of the pupils sing correctly.]

8	Do
7	Si
6	La
5	Sol
4	Fa
3	Mi
2	Re
1	Do

T. I am glad to hear so many of you sing so well. These eight sounds are called "The Scale," or "Musical Ladder." They are named from the lowest sound upwards, thus: One, Two, Three, Four, Five, Six, Seven, and Eight. Instead of writing the names out in full, it is usual to write only the figures, 1, 2, 3, 4, 5, 6, 7, and 8. I have drawn eight lines, one above another, to represent the Scale or Music-Ladder, and have written the figures upon the lines; also, the syllables Do, Re, Mi, Fa, Sol, La, Si, Do, which are sometimes sung instead of the Scale-names, as they sound better. As soon as you know the sounds of the Scale well enough, you should be able to sing any sound with the syllable La, or any other syllable, when called for.

These eight sounds of the scale not only differ in pitch, but they may also differ in length. We are at present enabled to tell the pitch of a sound by its scale-name, and also by its syllable.

We need now to be able to tell how long to sing a sound. If the class will be very attentive, I will try to show them how to do this by means of beating the time.

LESSON II.

DICTATION-EXERCISES UPON THE SCALE,

WITH BEATING TIME.

TWO—PART MEASURE.— SOUNDS ONE BEAT LONG.

Teacher. You may all rest, now, and listen to me; but be very attentive, and notice what I do.

[Teacher beats and sings.]

1.

La la la la la la la la la la la la la la la la.

T. What did I do?

Pupils. You sang two of each of the sounds of the scale.

T. You may sing as I did, beating the time.

[It is done correctly.]

T. That was well done. You may sing the scale downward, beginning with Eight, in the same way as you sang it upward.

[The pupils do it correctly.]

T. I fear you will become tired if you sing all the time; so I will form the class in two divisions, in order that one division may rest while the other sings.

Those on my right we will call the First Division, and those on my left, the Second Division.

I wish you to sing the scale up and down in this way, namely: the First Division to sing the first measure, and the Second Division to sing the second measure, and so on.

You must continue to beat the time, whether you sing or not. In this way each division will rest during every other measure.

Now ! all ready, and see if you understand what I want you to do.

[Enough of the pupils in each division understand so as to do it very well.]

T. You have done that much better than I thought you could.

SOUNDS TWO BEATS LONG.

T. You may all rest, now, and listen to me. Notice what I do.

[Teacher beats and sings.]

P. You sang each sound of the scale two beats long.
T. You may beat and sing as I did.

[Pupils beat and sing correctly.]

SOUNDS ONE BEAT AND TWO BEATS LONG.

T. Listen to me again, and tell me if I sing something new.

[The pupils will not comprehend this so readily as the exercises presented before. If they fail to understand by singing La, the teacher may sing the syllables. This will make it easier to perceive that the first three sounds are of the same pitch, and so on; then the pupils will be able to turn their attention to the difference in length. Lead them to know that there are *three Ones*, the first two being each one beat long, the third two beats long, and so of the other sounds of the scale.

Require the pupils, first to sing the exercise by the scale-names; second, by the syllables. Have the pupils sing by divisions,— two measures each. If not too tiresome, have the exercise sung downward, repeating the Eight.

If the pupils have not become quite proficient in beating two-part measure at this stage, it will be well to give further special attention in this direction before proceeding to the next lesson, which is in triple time; as a proper performance of beating three-part measure will depend largely upon their proficiency in two-part measure.]

LESSON III.

DEVELOPMENT OF THREE-PART MEASURE.

T. Who can tell what I sing now, that is different from anything I have sung before.

[Teacher sings.]

P. You sang three, of every sound of the scale.

T. Yes. I will sing the same again, and you may tell me which one of the three I sing loud.

[Teacher sings.]

P. You sang the first of the three loud, and the other two soft.

T. Yes. You may sing as I did.

[Pupils sing correctly.]

T. That is right. This kind of measure, with three parts—one loud and two soft—is called a three-part measure.

LESSON IV.

SPECIAL DRILL IN BEATING TRIPLE-TIME.

T. In three-part measure, there are three different motions of the hand. The first beat is the same as in two-part measure. The second beat is made by bringing the hand smartly to the left, so as to touch the body. The third beat brings the hand into position for the down beat of the following measure.

[The pupils are to practise this kind of measure, saying, while beating, Down, Left, Up, till the class can do it perfectly, accenting the down-beat. When this is accomplished, they will be able to do the following dictation exercises.]

EXERCISES IN THE SCALE WITH TRIPLE TIME.

T. I will sing the last exercise while beating, then I want you to do it.

[The teacher sings the exercise and the pupils do the same, being careful to accent the down-beat.]

T. That is very well. Now you may sing it, by divisions, one measure at a time, up and down the scale.

[This is done correctly.]

LESSON V.

FOUR–PART MEASURE.

T. You may sing four of each of the sounds of the scale, by the syllables.

[The pupils sing.]

T. That is very well. You may sing the same exercise again, and accent the first and *third* sounds in each measure, the first a little louder than the third.

[The pupils sings the exercise very well. The leading singers show that they *feel the time*, or recurrence of the accent,—some by an extravagant nod of the head, some by throwing forward the whole body, and others by stamping their feet,— all quite unconsciously.]

T. You observed the accented parts very well; but it was very funny to see the different motions you made as you became interested in keeping the time. Regular practice in beating the time, will prevent these awkward motions of the body and stamping of feet.

[The pupils may now take position for beating four-part measure.]

T. The four beats in Quadruple Time; are: Down, Left, Right, and Up.

The Down beat is made the same as in double and triple time, by bringing the tip of the middle finger of the right hand into the centre of the palm of the left.

The Left-beat is made like that of triple time.

The Right-beat is made by bringing the fingers of the right hand from the body onto the *fingers* of the left hand.

The Up-beat is made by bringing the hand up again to the position for making the Down-beat.

Now sing— by the syllables—the last exercise, beating the time.

The pupils do as directed.

T. Now sing by divisions, up and down.

[The pupils do it correctly.]

T. I am very glad you have become so much interested in learning how to sing the scale, in the different kinds of time, that you have not asked for any songs. If you go on in this way, you will soon be able to read music well enough to learn songs by the notes, without having ever heard them sung before.

READING MUSIC FROM FIGURES.

EXPLANATORY.

Pupils are supposed to have already had so much explanation and practice in the major scale as to be able to sing the sounds in order, ascending and descending; also to sing any sound of the scale by the syllables, when called by the teacher. In dictation-exercises, the teacher should *always* call the sounds by the scale-names, but the pupils should sing the syllables in response.

They are also supposed to have been taught:— Double time, including the manner of beating the same, as Down-beat and Up-beat, accenting the Down-beat; Triple-time, with the manner of beating the same,— Down-beat, Left-beat and Up-beat, accenting the Down-beat; Quadruple-time, with the manner of beating the same,—Down-beat, Left-beat, Right-beat and Up-beat, accenting the Down- and Right-beats.

For convenience in reading music, the measures are indicated by vertical lines called bars. At the end of an exercise or tune, two lines are used, called a double-bar.

Pupils are now told that, instead of the teacher calling the sounds of the scale, they are to sing from the figures, 1, 2, 3, 4, 5, 6, 7, and 8. This will be reading the sounds of the scale by figures.

As to the length of sounds, they are to be made to understand:—

(1.) That a figure with a comma after it means that the sound is to be one beat long.

(2.) That a figure with a dash after it means that the sound is to be two beats long.

(3.) That a cipher with a comma after it means that we are to rest, or keep silent, one beat; and a dash after a cipher means that we are to rest during two beats.

By this arrangement of figures, with commas and dashes after them, we know which sound of the scale to sing, and how long to sing it; also, how many beats to rest or keep silent.

The teacher will explain the above from the blackboard, and then practise from the books.

What makes it more difficult to read music than it is to read common language is, that in reading music you have to think of two things at the same time:—

First, you have to think which sound of the scale you are to sing.

Second, you must think how long you are to sing each sound; so that learning to read music correctly and intelligently causes us to think quickly, and do things accurately, more than any other study.

Third, if you sing the words of a song or exercise, instead of singing the scale-names or syllables, Do, Re, Mi, Fa, etc., it increases the difficulty very much. For that reason, you should practise easy music with words, that you may overcome the difficulties all by yourselves. You should also have credit for it, as well as in your other studies.

THE FIRST TWO SOUNDS OF THE SCALE.— TWO-PART MEASURE.

1.
1, 1, | 2, 0, | 2, 2, | 1, 0, ‖ **2.** 1, 1, | 2, 2, | 1, 2, | 1, 0, ‖

3.
1, 1, | 1, 0, | 2, 2, | 2, 0, | 1, 2, | 1, 1, | 2, 2, | 1, 0, ‖
Love-ly May,   Love-ly May,   Drives the chill-ing winds a - way.

COMMENCING WITH THE UP-BEAT.

4.
1, | 1, 2, | 1, 1, | 2, 1, | 2, 2, | 1, 2, | 1, 1, | 2, 2, | 1, ‖
I saw the smil-ing, gold-en sun, Sink to his rest when day was done.

THE FIRST THREE SOUNDS OF THE SCALE.

5.
1, 2, | 3, 0, | 3, 2, | 1, 0, ‖ **6.** 1, 2, | 3, 2, | 3, 2, | 1, 0, ‖

7.
1, 2, | 3, 0, | 3, 2, | 3, 0, | 3, 2, | 1, 2, | 3, 2, | 1, 0, ‖

8.
1, 2, | 3, 0, | 2, 3, | 2, 0, | 1, 2, | 3, 2, | 3, 2, | 1, 0, ‖

9.
3, 2, | 1, 0, | 2, 3, | 2, 0, | 3, 3, | 2, 2, | 1, 2, | 1, 0, ‖

10.

1, 1, | 2, 2, | 3, 2, | 3, 0, | 3, 3, | 2, 2, | 3, 2, | 1, 0, ‖

Work with God up - on thy side; This will keep thy heart from pride.

COMMENCING WITH THE UP-BEAT.

11.

1, | 2, 1, | 2, 2, | 3, 2, | 3, 3, | 2, 1, | 2, 3, | 2, 2, | 1 ‖

12.

1, | 1, 2, | 3, 3, | 2, 1, | 2, 2, | 3, 2, | 1, 2, | 3, 2, | 1, ‖

Come, one and all, a-round me stand, And praise our goodly na - tive land.

SKIPPING OVER TWO OF THE SCALE.

13.   **14. ℗**

1, 2, | 3, 0, | 3, 2, 1, 0, ‖ 1, 3, | 2, 2, | 1, 3, | 1, 0, ‖

15.

1, 1, | 2, 0, | 2, 2, | 3, 0, | 3, 2, | 3, 1, | 2, 2, | 1, 0, ‖

Bells do ring, bells do ring, In the for est birds do sing.

THE FIRST FOUR SOUNDS OF THE SCALE.

16.   **℗**

1, 2, | 3, 0, | 3, 4, | 3, 0, | 3, 4, | 3, 2, | 1, 2, | 1, 0, ‖

17.

1, 2, | 3, 0, | 2, 3, | 4, 0, | 3, 2, | 1, 3, | 2, 2, | 1, 0, ‖

Sun-shine bright, Sun-shine bright, Comes to fill us with de - light.

SOUNDS TWO BEATS LONG.

18.

1- | 1, 1, | 2- | 2, 2, | 3, 3, | 4, 3, | 2, 2, 1 ‖

19.

1- | 1, 1, | 2, 2, | 3, 0, | 4- | 3, 3, | 2, 2, | 1, 0, ‖

Hark! to the bu - gle call, Hark! how it sum-mons all.

SKIPPING FROM ONE TO THREE, TWO TO FOUR, THREE TO ONE, AND ONE TO FOUR.

20.   **21. ℗**

1, 3, | 2, 4, | 3, 2, | 1- ‖ 3, 1, | 4, 3, | 2, 2, | 1- ‖

22.

1, 3, | 1, 0, | 2, 4, | 2, 0, | 3, 1, | 4, 3, | 2, 2, | 1– ‖

Fair Spring days,   Joy - ous days,   Give for them to God all praise.

COMMENCING WITH THE UP-BEAT.

23.

1, | 1, 2, | 3, 1, | 2, 3, | 4, 2, | 3, 2, | 1, 3, | 2, 2, | 1, ‖

The   sun to cheer us brings the day, And bless-es with his set-ting ray.

THE FIRST FIVE SOUNDS OF THE SCALE.

24.

1, 2, | 3, 2, | 3, 4, | 5, 0, | 5, 4, | 3, 4, | 3, 2, | 1, 0, ‖

25.

1, 2, | 3– | 3, 4, | 5– | 4, 4, | 3, 3, | 2, 2, | 1– ‖

Trust in God, trust in God, Who all bless-ings pours a - broad.

TRIPLE OR THREE-PART MEASURE.

26.

1, 1, 1, | 2, 2, 2, | 3, 3, 4, | 5– 0, | 4, 4, 4, |

3, 3, 3, | 2, 3, 2, | 1– 0, ‖

27.

1, 1, 2, | 3, 3, 4, | 5, 4, 3, | 2– 0, | 2, 3, 4, |

See how the set - ting sun fades in the west ! Birds of the

5, 4, 3, | 4, 3, 2, | 1– 0, ‖

green-wood are gone to their rest.

COMMENCING WITH THE UP-BEAT.

28.

1, | 1, 2, 3, | 4– 3, | 2, 3, 4, | 5– 5, | 4, 3, 2, |

1– 3, | 2, 3, 2, | 1– ‖

29.

1, | 1, 2, 3, | 2, 0, 2, | 2, 3, 4, | 3, 0, 3, | 2, 3, 4, |

Thou star of the night, So high and so bright, I gaze on thy

5, 5, 4, | 3, 3, 2, | 1, 0, ‖

beau - ty with heart-felt de - light.

SKIPPING OVER TWO AND FOUR.

30.   **31.**

1, 3, | 5– | 5, 3, | 1– ‖ 1, 3, | 5, 3, | 4, 2, | 1– ‖

32.

1, 1, 3, | 5, 0, 0, | 1, 1, 3, | 5, 0, 0, | 4, 3, 2, |
Let us join hands,   Let us join hands,   This pledge of

3, 1, 3, | 5, 4, 2, | 1, 0, 0, ‖
love friendship ev - er de - mands.

33.   **P**

1, 2, | 3, 1, | 4, 1, | 5, 0, | 5, 4, | 3, 5, | 2, 5, | 1, 0, ‖

34.

1, 1, 2, | 3, 2, 1, | 5, 4, 3, | 2– 0, | 2, 3, 4, |
Let ev - 'ry crea - ture sing praise to the Lord,   Let ev - 'ry

5, 3, 1, | 4, 3, 2, | 1– 0, ‖
crea - ture sing praise to the Lord.

THE FIRST SIX SOUNDS OF THE SCALE.

35.   **P**

1, 2, | 3, 4, | 5, 6, | 5, 0, | 6, 5, | 4, 3, | 2, 2, | 1, 0, ‖

36.

1, 2, | 3, 3, | 2, 2, | 1, 1, | 3, 4, | 5, 5, | 4, 4, | 3, 0, ‖
Kind, pro - tect-ing God in heav-en, Good-ness from thee ev - er flows;

2, 3, | 4, 4, | 3, 4, | 5, 5, | 6, 6, | 5, 4, | 3, 2, | 1, 0, ‖
Thou has sent me sweet-est slumber, Strengthen'd me with sweet re - pose.

QUADRUPLE OR FOUR-PART MEASURE.

37.

1, 2, 3, 4, | 5, 5, 5, 5, | 4, 3, 2, 1, | 2, 2, 2, 0, |
Tho' my cot be poor and scan-ty, 'T is a hap - py home for me;

2, 3, 4, 5, | 6, 6, 6, 6, | 5, 4, 3, 2, | 1, 1, 1, 0, ‖
I shall dwell in peace and plen- ty, If my soul con - tent-ed be.

38.
1, 3, 5, 0, | 1, 4, 6, 0, | 1, 5, 6, 4, | 2, 5, 1, 0, ‖

39.
1, 3, 5, 3, | 4, 6, 5, 0, | 1, 3, 5, 3, | 4, 6, 5, 0, ‖
Birds that in the for - est throng, Sing a joy-ful, hap-py song :

6, 4, 2, 0, | 5, 3, 1, 0, | 4, 2, 3, 1, | 5, 5, 1, 0, ‖
Sing with glee, all the day, In the love-ly month of May.

ALL THE EIGHT SOUNDS OF THE SCALE.

40.
1, 2, | 3, 4, | 5, 6, | 7, 8, | 8, 7, | 6, 5, | 4, 3, | 2, 1, ‖

41.
1, 2, | 3, 2, | 3, 4, | 5, 0, | 6, 7, | 8, 7, | 6, 7, | 8, 0, ‖

42.
1, | 3, 2, 3, 4, | 5– 3, 8, | 7, 6, 5, 4, | 3– 0, ‖
When will the winds be soft - er, When will the fields be green,

5, | 8, 7, 6, 5, | 5– 3, 5, | 6, 4, 3, 2, | 1– 0, ‖
Come May thou love-ly lin - g'rer, We'll hail you for our queen.

TWO–PART SINGING.

Divide the class into two equal parts, taking care to have a few of the leading voices on each part. Beat the time with care.

43.

FIRST DIVISION.	0, 0,	3, 3,	0, 0,	3, 3,	0, 0,	4, 3,	2, 2,	1–
SECOND DIVISION.	1, 2,	0, 0,	1, 2,	0, 0,	4, 3,	0, 0,	2, 2,	1–

44.

FIRST DIVISION.	3, 3,	2, 2,	0, 0,	0–	4, 4,	3, 3,	0, 0,	0–
SECOND DIVISION.	0, 0,	0, 0,	1, 1,	1–	0, 0,	0, 0,	2, 2,	2–

3, 4,	5, 4,	0, 0,	0, 0,	0, 0,	5, 4,	3, 2,	1–
0, 0,	0, 0,	3, 3,	2–	3, 4,	0, 0,	3, 2,	1–

45.

FIRST DIVISION.	0, 0,	0, 0,	5, 6,	7, 8,	0, 0,	0, 0,	4, 3,	2, 1,
SECOND DIVISION.	1, 2,	3, 4,	0, 0,	7, 8,	8, 7,	6, 5,	0, 0,	2, 1,

46.

FIRST DIVISION.	0, 0,	0, 0,	1, 3,	5–	0, 0,	0, 0	5, 3,	1–
SECOND DIVISION.	1, 1,	3, 3,	0, 0,	0–	5, 5,	3, 3	0, 0,	1–

47.   ?

FIRST DIVISION.	8, 8,	7, 7,	0, 0,	0–	0, 0,	0, 0,	5, 3,	2–
SECOND DIVISION.	0, 0,	0, 0,	6, 6,	5–	5, 5,	6, 5,	0, 0,	0–

	0, 0,	0, 0,	3, 4,	5–	0, 0,	0, 0,	6, 7,	8–
	2, 3,	4, 4,	0, 0,	0–	5, 5,	6, 5,	6, 7,	8–

48.

FIRST DIVISION.	5, 3,	6, 4,	5, 3,	6–	0, 0,	0, 0,	0, 0,	0–
SECOND DIVISION.	0, 0,	0, 0,	0, 0,	0–	5, 3,	6, 4,	5, 3,	6–

	5, 3,	0, 0,	6, 4,	0, 0,	3, 6,	5, 4,	3, 2,	1–
	0, 0,	5, 3,	0, 0,	6, 4,	3, 6,	5, 4,	3, 2,	1–

REGULAR NOTATION.

The foregoing plan, of reading only by the figures or syllables of the scale, does very well to begin with; but you should soon outgrow this grade of musical existence, as a frog outgrows the tadpole and breathes no longer as a fish, but with head out of water.

All you have learned of the scale and measures in the preceding lessons we shall retain; and it will aid you very much to understand the reading of music by the regular notation. We will add to the scale diagram the pitch-names of each sound.

LESSON I.

THE LETTERS AND G-CLEF.

8	$\bar{\bar{c}}$	Do
7	$\bar{b}$	Si
6	$\bar{a}$	La
5	$\bar{g}$	Sol
4	$\bar{f}$	Fa
3	$\bar{e}$	Mi
2	$\bar{d}$	Re
1	$\bar{c}$	Do

(1.) The pitch of sounds is named by the first seven letters of the alphabet: *a, b, c, d, e, f,* and *g.*

(2.) You see by the diagram, that the pitch of One is *c*; Two is *d*; Three is *e*; Four is *f*; Five is *g*; Six is *a*; Seven is *b*; and Eight is *c*.

(3.) You will notice that *c* is used as the pitch for both One and Eight. We distinguish the *c*'s by the number of marks over them; the pitch of One is called "once-marked *c*" and of Eight, "twice-marked *c*."

(4.) Upon the fifth degree of the scale you will observe this character, which is called the $\bar{g}$-Clef or Key, and always stands for that letter or pitch.

We have already sung exercises in three kinds of measures: Two-part measures, Three-part measures, and Four-part measures.

You will need no further instruction about measures for our present practice; only you must remember that the first tick or count of every measure is louder than the others; or, is "accented."

LESSON II.

NOTES AND RESTS.

I will explain to you the different kinds of notes used to show the difference in the length of sounds; also the rests, which show how long to be silent. This is best shown by four-part measures, in the following manner:—

T. Tell me how many La's I sing while drawing the circle.

[Teacher makes a circle while she sings, thus:]

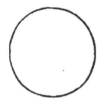 

La la la la.

P. Four.

[Teacher makes the dividing lines, thus:]

T. I have divided the circle into four equal parts. What is each part called?

P. A quarter.

[Teacher points to each quarter while she sings.]

La la la la.

T. How long was that sound which I sang to each quarter?

P. One tick or count.

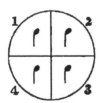

[Teacher places a quarter-note in each quarter of the circle, thus:]

T. I will write a note in each quarter which shall stand for a sound one tick or count, and will name them *Quarter Notes*.

T. You may tell me how many sounds I sing while drawing another circle.

[Teacher draws and sings:]

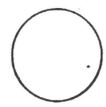 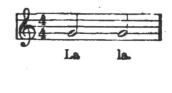

P. Two — each two quarters long.
T. I see you comprehend what I am "up to."

[Teacher, dividing the circle into halves by a horizontal line, and then into quarters by dots vertically, places half-notes upon the dotted lines dividing the quarters, thus:]

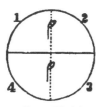 *T.* I have placed a note, as you see, above the line which divides the circle into halves, and which stands for a sound as long as two quarters; also, one under the line for the other two quarters. What name will you give to these notes?

P. Half-notes.
T. How many quarters do you sing to a half-note?
P. Two.

[Teacher draws a circle and sings :]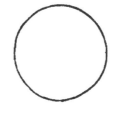

T. How many sounds did I sing in this circle?
P. One.

[Teacher divides the circle into quarters by dots, and places a whole note in the centre, thus:]

 *T.* This note lasts through all the four quarters. If we call the notes in the first circle *quarter-notes* and those in the second, *half-notes*, what name shall we give to this last note?
P. A *whole-note.*

T.   Yes.   Only the most attentive will be able to tell me how many I sing in the next circle.

[Teacher draws a circle, divides it into quarters, and sings.]

La   la   la   la   la   la   la   la.

P.   Eight!

[Teacher divides each quarter, thus:]

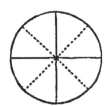

T.   Yes: I sang two sounds to each quarter.   You sing two sounds to each quarter while I point.

[Pupils sing correctly.]

T.   How many equal parts in this circle?
P.   Eight.
T.   I will write the notes, *two* of which are equal to one quarter.

[Teacher writes an eighth-note in each part, and asks:]

T.   Can you tell me the name of these notes?

[Pupils will probably give the right name; if not, tell them.]

T.   I will name each of these eight parts in a way which will be easy for you to tell.   I will name the first part of each quarter of the circles just as we did in the first circle, and the second part of each quarter we will call "&."

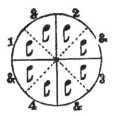

[Teacher writes.]

T.   We have four different kinds of notes.   I will place the circles all in a row, and will place the notes on a line under them.

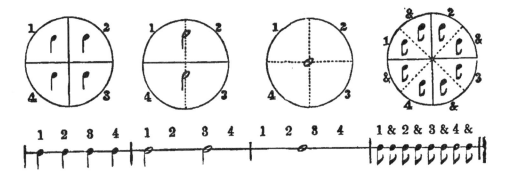

LESSON III.

RESTS.

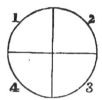 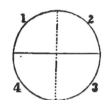 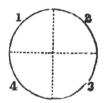 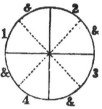

[Teacher draws four circles, divides them as above, and proceeds as follows.]

T.   Notice which parts I sing, and which parts I rest.

[Teacher sings the first and third parts.]

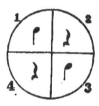

P.   You sang at the first and third parts, and rested at the second and fourth parts.

T.   I will write a quarter-note in the parts where I sang, and a quarter-rest where I rested.

[Teacher writes in the first circle.]

T.   Tell me which parts I sing in the next circle.

[Teacher, pointing, sings the first two quarters and rests the last two.]

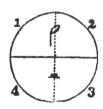

P.   You sang the first half, and rested the other half.

T.   Yes; and I will write a half-note for the first two quarters, and a half-rest for the last two.

[Teacher writes in the second circle.]

I will write a whole-rest in the third circle, which shows you are to rest during the four quarters.

[Teacher writes in the third circle.]

You will observe that the half-rest is above the line, and that the whole-rest is below the line.

T. Tell me which parts I sing, in the first two quarters of the fourth circle, and in which I rest.

[Teacher sings.]

P. You sang *one* and *two*, and rested at the &'s.

T. I will write eighth-notes where I sang, and eighth-rests where I rested. I will commence again, and sing all around, and you notice how I sing the third and fourth quarters.

[Teacher writes, and again sings.]

P. You sang both parts in the third quarter, and sang the first part of the fourth quarter, and rested on the &.

[Teacher writes in the remaining divisions of the fourth circle.]

T. Under the four circles containing rests I will place the notes and rests, on a line.

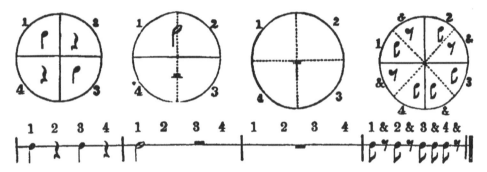

THE STAFF.

Music is written upon five lines and the spaces between the lines. The lines and spaces. called the Staff, are named from the lowest upwards, thus:

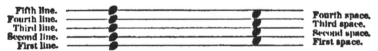

Fifth line.		Fourth space.
Fourth line.		Third space.
Third line.		Second space.
Second line.		First space.
First line.		

Sometimes the spaces below and above the staff, and also short added lines are used, thus:

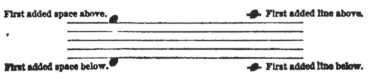

First added space above. — First added line above.

First added space below. — First added line below.

THE NEW SECOND NATIONAL MUSIC READER

" The Old and the New — Always the Best.'

THE NEW SECOND

NATIONAL MUSIC READER.

PART I.—READING AT SIGHT FROM THE STAFF.

EXERCISES ON THE SOUNDS OF THE SCALE.*

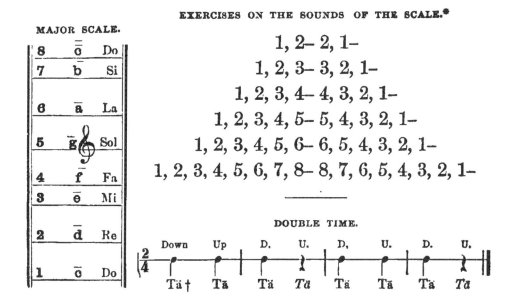

MAJOR SCALE.

1, 2– 2, 1–
1, 2, 3– 3, 2, 1–
1, 2, 3, 4– 4, 3, 2, 1–
1, 2, 3, 4, 5– 5, 4, 3, 2, 1–
1, 2, 3, 4, 5, 6– 6, 5, 4, 3, 2, 1–
1, 2, 3, 4, 5, 6, 7, 8– 8, 7, 6, 5, 4, 3, 2, 1–

DOUBLE TIME.

THE SCALE UPON THE STAFF, ASCENDING AND DESCENDING.

Scale-Names.	1	2	3	4	5	6	7	8	8	7	6	5	4	3	2	1
Pitch-Names.	c	d	e	f	g	a	b	c	c	b	a	g	f	e	d	c
Syllables.	Do	Re	Mi	Fa	Sol	La	Si	Do	Do	Si	La	Sol	Fa	Mi	Re	Do

* A comma after a figure means a short sound; a dash, a long sound.

† Those desiring to use the Time-Names, should carefully read the Appendix, p. 179. It has been expressed by many able teachers, that those schools which for the next five years shall in their exercises require *beating time with the hand*, with the proper use of the Time-Names, will excel in "Sight-Singing." The author can testify to a trial of them for three years in Japan, under the most favorable circumstances for testing their value, with results in the highest degree satisfactory.

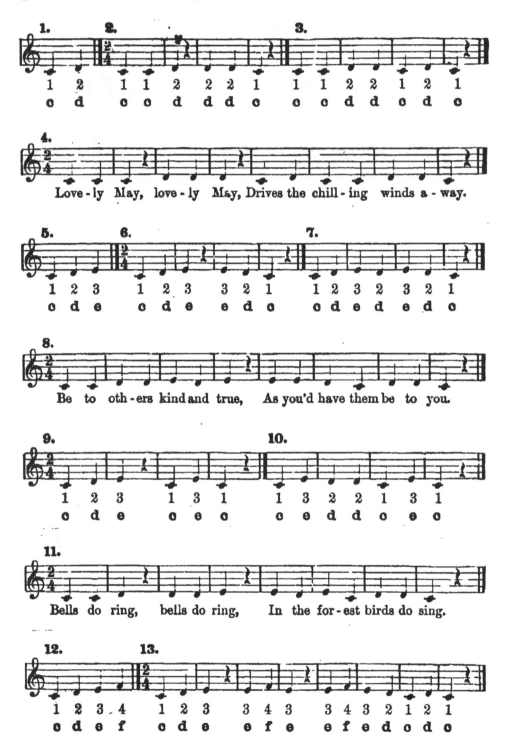

14.

Sun-shine bright, sun-shine bright, Comes to fill us with de-light.

SOUNDS LASTING ONE MEASURE.

15.

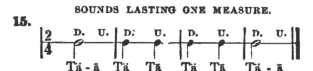

When a sound lasts during two beats in double time, as in the first and last measures in the above exercise, it is named Tä-ä: the vowel sound is changed *with the up-beat,* and the consonant is omitted.

16.

Hark to the bu-gle call; Hark! how it sum-mons all!

17.   **18.**

1 3 2 4 3 2 1   3 1 4 3 2 2 1
c e d f e d c   e c f e d d c

19.

Fair spring days, joy-ous days! Give for them to God all praise.

COMMENCING WITH THE UP-BEAT.

20.

When exercises and songs commence with the up-beat, do not beat several measures before commencing to sing the notes or say the time-names; but *begin at once,* with the up-beat.

21.

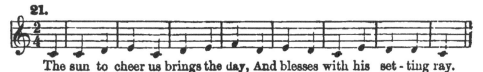

The sun to cheer us brings the day, And blesses with his set-ting ray.

1 2 3 4 5   1 2 3 2 3 4 5   5 4 3 4 3 2 1
c d e f g   c d e d e f g   g f e f e d c

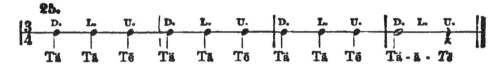

Trust in God, trust in God, Who all bless-ings pours a-broad.

TRIPLE OR THREE-PART MEASURE.

D. L. U. D. L. U. D. L. U. D. L. U.
Tä Tä Tē Tä Tä Tē Tä Tä Tē Tä - ä · Tē

BEATING TRIPLE TIME.

Have the class take position for beating time.

The down-beat is made the same as the down-beat in double time. The left-beat is made by bringing the hand smartly against the body, *and holding it there*, till the time comes to make the up-beat, which is done by bringing the hand quickly to the position for making the down-beat again.

See how the set-ting sun fades in the west,

See how the set-ting sun fades in the west!

Let us sing a mer-ry lay; Sing we ev-er while we may.

COMMENCING WITH THE UP-BEAT.

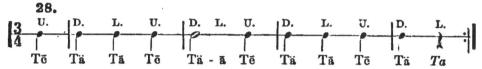

28.

This is an exercise in beating triple time, commencing with the up-beat. Let the hand be placed firmly against the body before commencing; then commence promptly, by a sign from the teacher.

29.

Thou star of the night, so high and so bright,

I gaze on thy beau - ty with heart - felt de - light.

30.   **31.**

1 3 5 5 3 1   1 3 5 3 4 2 1

c e g g e c   c e g e f d c

32.

Tä Tä Tō Tä Tä Tē Tä Tä Tō Tä Tä Tē

33.

Let us join hands, Let us join hands;

This pledge of love, friend-ship ev - er de - mands.

34.

1 2 3 1 4 1 5   5 4 3 5 2 5 1

c d e c f c g   g f e g d g c

*The question-mark will always indicate a point requiring special attention.

SOUNDS LASTING ONE MEASURE.

In saying Tä-ä-ĕ, the sound is started with the down-beat, and the vowel sounds are changed *with* the left- and up-beats; the consonants being omitted.

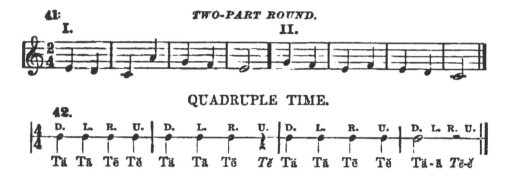

QUADRUPLE TIME.

In No. 42 we have quadruple or four-part measure for the first time. It is better to designate the parts of measures by the order of the beats than by counting the time as in instrumental music; retaining the figures or numerals only to designate the degrees or sounds of the scale.

MANNER OF BEATING QUADRUPLE TIME.

1. Take position for beating time.
2. The down-and left-beats are performed as in triple time. The right-beat is made by bringing the right hand from the body to the fingers of the left hand. The up-beat is made like the up-beat in double time.

The advantages on the score of discipline will abundantly compensate for the trouble of securing strict uniformity in beating time, apart from its use in the study of music.

Let the teacher persevere in this matter till the pupils can do it well.

THE TIME-NAMES IN QUADRUPLE TIME.

The time-names in quadruple or four-part measure are : —

For the Down-beat, Ta : *a* as in far.
For the Left-beat, Tä : *a* as in fate.
For the Right-beat, Tē : *e* as in mē.
For the Up-beat, Tĕ : *e* as in mĕt.

Quadruple time is accented on the down-and right-beats.

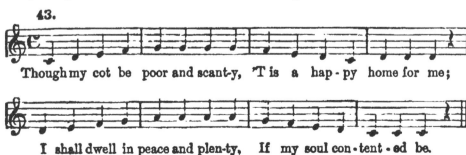

44.

```
1   3   5     1   4   6     1   5   6   4   2   5   1
c   e   g     c   f   a     c   g   a   f   d   g   c
```

45.

Birds that in the for-est throng Sing a joy-ful, hap-py song:

Sing with glee all the day, In the love-ly month of May.

46.

```
1   2   3   4   5   6   7   8   8   7   6   5   4   3   2   1
c   d   e   f   g   a   b   c   c   b   a   g   f   e   d   c
```

47.

```
1   2   3   2   3   4   5   6   7   8   7   6   7   8
c   d   e   d   e   f   g   a   b   c   b   a   b   c
```

48.

Time by mo-ments steals a-way, First the hour and then the day;

Small the dai-ly loss ap-pears, Yet it soon a-mounts to years.

EXERCISES IN FIGURES, TO BE WRITTEN IN NOTES.

EXPLANATION.—A comma after a figure, signifies a quarter-note, thus: 1,═♩

A dash after a figure, signifies a half-note, thus: 1- ═♩

A comma after a cipher, stands for a quarter-rest, thus: 0,═𝄽

A dash after a cipher, stands for a half-rest, thus: 0- ═ ▬

The key in which the exercise is to be written is denoted by a capital letter, and the time, by the usual signature.

EXAMPLES.

I.

C. 2/4 1, 2, | 3- | 3, 4, | 5,- | 5, 4, | 3- | 3, 2, | 1- ‖

Written in notes upon the staff, appears thus:

II.

C. 2/4 1, 2, | 3, 0, | 3, 4, | 5, 0, | 5, 1, | 5, 1, | 5, 5, | 1, 0, |

In notes, thus:

III.

C. 2/4 1, 3, | 1, 3, | 2, 5, | 5, 0, | 5, 3, | 5, 3, | 2, 3, | 1, 0, |

IV.

C. 2/4 1, 2, | 3, 4, | 5- | 6- | 5, 6, | 5, 4, | 3, 2, | 1- ‖

V.

C. 2/4 1, 3, | 2, 4, | 3, 5, | 5- | 6, 4, | 2, 5, | 3, 1, | 1- ‖

VI.

C. 2/4 3, 1, | 4, 2, | 3, 5, | 1- | 6, 4, | 2, 4, | 3, 2, | 1- ‖

VII.

C. 2/4 3, 5, | 4, 6, | 5, 3, | 3- | 4, 2, | 3, 1, | 2, 3, | 1- ‖

VIII.

C. $\frac{4}{4}$ 1, 2, 3, 4, | 5- 3- | 4, 5, 6, 7, | 8- 0- | 8, 7, 6, 5, | 4- 3- |
5, 4, 3, 2, | 1- 0- |

IX.

C. $\frac{3}{4}$ 1, 1, 1, | 1, 0, 0, | 2, 2, 2, | 2, 0, 0, | 3, 4, 5, | 5, 4, 3, |
2, 3, 2, | 1, 0, 0, |

X.

C. $\frac{3}{4}$ 1, 2, 3, | 1, 0, 0, | 3, 3, 4, | 5, 0, 0, | 5, 4, 3, | 5, 4, 3, |
2, 3, 2, | 1, 0, 0, |

XI.

C. $\frac{3}{4}$ 5, 5, 5, | 5, 0, 0, | 3, 3, 3, | 3, 0, 0, | 4, 3, 2, | 4, 3, 2, |
3, 4, 2, | 1, 0, 0, |

XII.

C. $\frac{3}{4}$ 1, 1, 3, | 5, 0, 0, | 1, 1, 3, | 5, 0, 0, | 4, 4, 4, | 3, 3, 3, |
2, 3, 2, | 1, 0, 0, |

XIII.

C. $\frac{3}{4}$ 1, 3, 1, | 5, 0, 0, | 1, 3, 1, | 5, 0, 0, | 4, 5, 4, | 3, 4, 3, |
2, 3, 2, | 1, 0, 0, |

XIV.

C. $\frac{3}{4}$ 3, 1, 3, | 5, 0, 0, | 3, 1, 3, | 5, 0, 0, | 3, 2, 1, | 5, 4, 3, |
4, 3, 2, | 1, 0, 0, |

XV.

C. $\frac{3}{4}$ 5, 3, 1, | 2, 0, 0, | 5, 3, 1, | 2, 0, 0, | 1, 3, 5, | 5, 3, 1, |
2, 3, 2, | 1, 0, 0, |

The pupils should sing the above exercises from the figures, beating the time, before writing them in notes. It is recommended that only one exercise be taken up at one lesson, in the following order, namely:

1. Teacher writes the exercise in figures upon the blackboard.
2. Pupils sing it by the (a) scale names, (b) pitch names, and (c) syllables.
3. Write the exercise in notes upon the staff.
4. Pupils pass their slates to each other, who examine and mark errors.

This should all be done in six or seven minutes, and is as good an intellectu exercise as arithmetic or grammar.

TRUST IN GOD.

MODERATO.

1. Tho' I wan-der blind-ly, Till in death I sleep,

God the Lord will kind-ly Me in safe-ty keep.

2 He whose love hath won me
Still to trust his care,
Will not put upon me
More than I can bear.

3 And should care oppress me,
Near him will I stay,
So his love shall bless me
Every coming day.

49.   50.

8 7 6 5 8 5 8   1 3 5 8 5 3 1
c b a g c g c   c e g c g e c

THE WATER-LILY.

MODERATE.

1. Be - side the blue lake there was stroll - ing one day,

A wil - ful young boy, all in - tent on his play.

2 And 'mid the green rushes he saw growing there
A beautiful lily, so white and so fair.

3 "Oh, that I must have!" cried he, eager with joy;
And into the lake went the heedless young boy.

4 "Stay, stay!" cried his mother, all trembling with fear,
"Oh, stay! for too deep is the water so clear."

5 He heeds not her bidding, he stays not to hear;
"No, no," answered he, "there is nothing to fear."

6 He grasped at the flower — but nothing could save;
He sank, and was lost in a watery grave.

* Take breath at this mark (') and at rests.

THREE EIGHTH-NOTES IN A MEASURE

THE DOTTED QUARTER IN THREE-EIGHT MEASURE.

52.

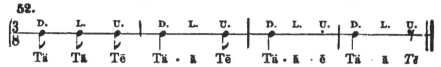

Tä   Tä   Tē   Tä · ä   Tē   Tä · ä · ē   Tä · ä   Tē

53.

Tä Tä Tē Tä-ä Tē Tä-ä Tē Tä-ä Tē Tä Tä Tē Tä-ä-ē Tä-ä Tē

54.

55.

LULLABY.

SOFT AND SLOW.

1. Gen - tly   to   sleep   I   sing thee,   Sing thee   to   peace - ful

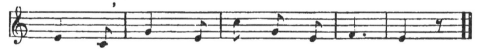

slum - ber;   Smile,   then,   while thou   art   sleep - ing.

2 Smile once again, I pray thee, closing thine eyes in slumber;
Sweetly sleep as I guard thee!

8 If thou wilt smile upon me when thou from sleep awakest,
We will play then together.

4 Sleep, for the angels keep thee, watching around thy cradle;
Sleep, and dream of the angels.

THE DOTTED QUARTER IN THREE-EIGHT MEASURE.

52.

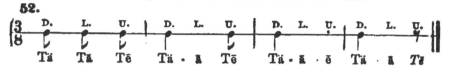

Tä   Tä   Tē   Tä - ä   Tē   Tä-ä - ē   Tä - ä   Tē

53.

Tä   Tä   Tē   Tä-ä Tē   Tä-ä Tē   Tä-ä Tē   Tä Tä Tē   Tä-ä-ē Tä-ä Tē

54.

55.

LULLABY.

SOFT AND SLOW.

1. Gen - tly   to   sleep   I   sing thee, Sing   thee   to   peace - ful

slum - ber;   Smile,   then,   while thou   art   sleep - ing.

2 Smile once again, I pray thee, closing thine eyes in slumber;
  Sweetly sleep as I guard thee !

3 If thou wilt smile upon me when thou from sleep awakest,
  We will play then together.

4 Sleep, for the angels keep thee, watching around thy cradle;
  Sleep, and dream of the angels.

THE SCALE EXTENDED UPWARDS FOUR SOUNDS.

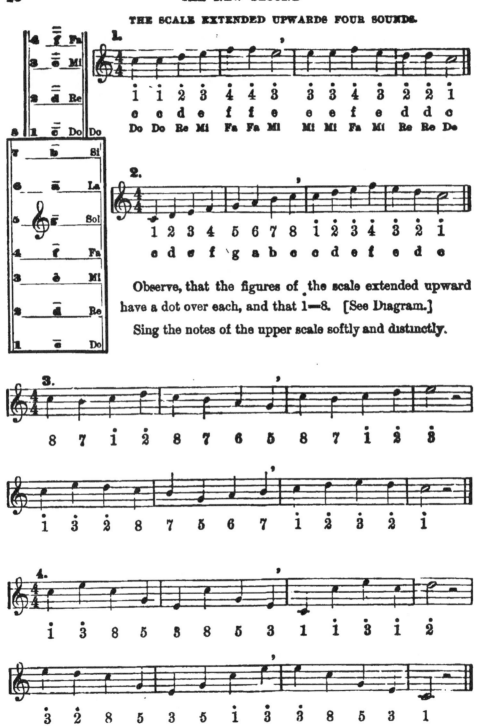

Observe, that the figures of the scale extended upward have a dot over each, and that 1—8. [See Diagram.]

Sing the notes of the upper scale softly and distinctly.

PRAISE OF SONG.

(May be pitched in B-flat or A.)

LIVELY.

1 Song doth the soul en · liv · en, And fill the heart with joy;
2 Then tune your cheer-ful voic es, Like birds that soar a · bove;

Yes! God the gift hath giv · en, Our sor · rows to de · stroy.
Let him whose heart re · joic · es, Sing songs of joy and love.

3 The bond that cannot perish,
   To friendship's bond, we 'll sing;
The brother that we cherish,
   The home to which we cling.

4 The man who 's ready ever
   To lend a helping arm;
The noble heart that never
   Will do his neighbor harm.

TWO SOUNDS OF EQUAL LENGTH IN EACH PART OF TWO-FOUR MEASURE.

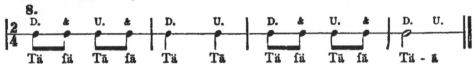

8.

When there are two sounds of equal length in each part of the measure in Double-time, they are named in their order, respectively, Tä, fä, Tä, fä, — as in the above exercise.

The pupil should be led to observe : —

1. When there are two sounds of equal length in one part of the measure, the first is sung *with* the beat, and the second *after* the beat; so, in the first measure in the above exercise,—

Tä comes *with* the down-beat,

fä comes *after* the down-beat,

Tä comes *with* the up-beat, and

fä comes *after* the up-beat; or,—

2. By another statement : when there are two sounds of equal length in either the first or second part of a measure in Double-time, the first of the two sounds comes *with the beat*, and the second *after the beat*.

9.

10.

11.

12.

A - men, A - men, A - men,   A - men, A - men, A - men.

WILMOT.

1. Heav'n-ly Fath - er, sov-'reign Lord, Be thy glo-rious name a - dored!
2. Tho' un - wor-thy, Lord, thine ear, Deign our hum-ble songs to hear;

Lord, thy mer - cies nev - er fail! Hail, ce- les- tial Good-ness, hail!
Pur- er praise we hope to bring, When a-round thy throne we sing.

3 While on earth ordained to stay,
Guide our footsteps in thy way,
Till we come to dwell with thee,
Till we all thy glory see.

4 Then with angel harps again,
We will wake a nobler strain;
There, in joyful songs of praise,
Our triumphant voices raise.

COMMENCING AFTER THE UP-BEAT; OR, ON fä.

13.

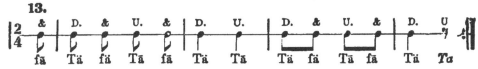

14.

THE SLY CAT.

GERMAN.

MODERATO.

1. Who on our wall is seat - ed? tra, la, la! Take
2. O spar-row, there's a watch - er! tra, la, la! There

care, or you'll be cheat - ed! tra, la, la, la! Oh, spar-row dear, take
sits the great mouse-catch-er! tra, la, la, la! So, spar-row dear, take

care, take care! The cat   is near! tra, la, la, la, la, la!
care, take care! The cat   is near! tra, la, la, la, la, la!

3 The cat is gone to rest now, tra, la, la!
    She knows the sparrow's nest, now, tra, la, la, la!
Oh, sparrow dear, take care, take care!
    The cat is near! tra, la, la, la, la, la!

4 The cat has caught a sparrow, tra, la, la!
    She flies now like an arrow, tra, la, la, la!
Oh, sparrow dear, the kittens there
    The feast will share! tra la, la, la, la, la!

FROM THREE-EIGHT TO SIX-EIGHT TIME.

All six-eight measures should be considered as being made up of two three-eight measures, as in the following example.

In the above example, the beats and Time-Names are the same for *a* and *b*. The chief difference between three-eight and six-eight time is in the accentuation. In three-eight time the accents are all alike. In six-eight time there are naturally two accents, the first being stronger than the second.

In quick six-eight measure, it is better to mark the time with two beats: the first half of the measure by a down- and the second by an up-beat, as above (*c*).

SIX-EIGHT MEASURE.

I.

Tä Tä Tē Tä Tä Tē Tä Tä Tē Tä-ä Tē Tä-ä Tē Ta Tä Tē Tä-ä-ē Tä-ä Tē

II.

III.

IV.

THE NIGHT IS GONE.

COMMENCING WITH Tē, AFTER THE UP-BEAT.

15.

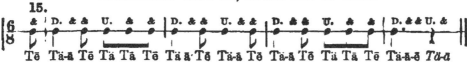

Tē Tä-ä Tē Tä Tä Tē Tä-ä Tē Tä-ä Tē Tä-ä Tē Tä Tä Tē Tä-ä-ē Tä-ä

MODERATE. (May be transposed to B-flat or A.) HOHMANN.

1. The night is gone, the day is here, And still I live and move
2. Lord, ev - 'ry bless-ing comes from thee, Thou who canst all things do!

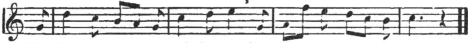

The God that gov-erns all the year, How con -stant is his love!
Oh, how much good dost thou to me From day to day re - new!

3 All that I do to thee is known,
  Who dost my wants supply;
My rising-up and lying-down
  Are subject to thine eye.

4 Should I in wisdom's ways be found,
  And strive to do the best,
Love shall encircle me around,
  And peace be in my breast.

The pupils should be led to see that, in the second measure, the dotted quarter-note lasts till the two beats are perfectly performed; and that the eighth-note which follows should be sung when the hand is at rest, *after* the up-beat.

16.

17.

COMMENCING AFTER THE UP—BEAT; OR, ON fä.

18.

19.

20.

BRISKLY WORK.

From the French.+

1. Out of bed with-out de-lay, Dream not in the light of day; Not a task nor

du-ty shirk, But with speed perform your work; Then en-joy the time for play

2 Briskly work; be wide awake;
  Care with all your duties take;
    Not a thing forget nor slight;
    What you do, pray do it right!
  Busy fingers light work make.

3 Briskly work, and little say;
  Move what e'er impedes the way;
    Seek at once for what you need;
    All the laws of order heed;
  So be happy all the day.

THE DOTTED QUARTER-NOTE IN FOUR-FOUR TIME.

COMMENCING WITH THE UP-BEAT; OR, ON Tĕ.

WINTER SONG.

BOLDLY.

1. Old Win - ter is a spir - it bold, No dan - ger can a -
2. If e'er a man was sound, 't is he : He pines and sick - ens

larm him; His bod - y is of i - ron mould, Nor sweet nor sour can
nev - er; From sore dis - eas - es he is free; He knows not pain nor

harm .. him, Nor sweet nor sour can ev - er harm him.
fe - ver, He knows not, knows not pain nor fe - ver.

3 He dons his garments out of doors, And lets no fire come near them;
At pains and aches he laughs and roars,—He hath no cause to fear them,
He hath no cause, no cause to fear them.

4 He cares not for the song of birds, Nor heeds the springing flower;
The cheering cup, warm hearts and words, To charm him have no power,
To charm him, charm him have no power.

5 But when the wolves are howling loud O'er frozen lake and river,
When round the blazing hearth we crowd, And rub our hands, and shiver,
And rub, and rub our hands, and shiver,—

6 When chilling storms are raging round, And frosty winds are blowing,—
That cheers his heart; he loves the sound; He laughs with joy o'erflowing,
He laughs with joy, with joy o'erflowing.

7 For at the north pole he resides, Where northern seas are swelling,
On Switzerland's high hills, besides, He has a summer dwelling,
He has a summer, summer dwelling.

8 So, to and fro, with all his band, He's marching, marching ever;
And when he passes by, we stand To gaze on him, and shiver,
To gaze, to gaze on him, and shiver.

THE SCALE EXTENDED DOWNWARD.

(Exercises from 1 to 6 may be pitched in D or E.)

Observe that the figures of the scale extended downward have the dots beneath, and that 8 = 1. [See Diagram.]

'Though dark night a - round us low - er, Let us not be - wail,

But con - fide in Heav-en's pow - er—That shall nev - er fail.

(The following exercise to be sung in exact pitch.)

PREPARATORY EXERCISES.

TWO-PART SINGING.

Divide the class into two equal parts, each part having an equal number of leading singers. This will be the first step in selecting the voices for two-part singing. Dr. A. B. MARX pursues a similar course without saying much about it. The pupils should beat the time.

If there are boys and girls in the class, let the girls form the first division and the boys the second. Then change parts, the boys singing very softly on the upper part.

3.

Great care should be taken that the first division sing very softly and distinctly. If any of the pupils cannot sing the upper notes easily, they must sing in the second division. If some of the pupils sing out of tune, they should listen a while, but care should be taken not to discourage them.

In the following exercise, the first division have three sounds of the upper scale and the second division have five sounds of the lower scale.

4.
SLOWLY.

Exercises like the above, will tend towards the acquirement of two important arts in reading music :

1. "Leading off" and "coming in."
2. Learning to listen to other parts while singing one's own.

LISTENING WHILE SINGING.

Each singer must be able to hear the other part, and follow its import, while he sings his own.

It is of no use to tell a pupil to mind his own business,—"to sing his part without thinking of the other." He *cannot* do it, because he is not deaf! If he could, it would not be desirable, as one part would be very apt to "outcry" the other: to sing out of tune and out of time with it. Besides, such a thing deprives a singer of the enjoyment of the harmony; and again, it prevents that union of feeling which is so essential to the proper expression of a piece. The ground-work of the ability to hear, enjoy, and execute "harmonic song" lies in the ability to hear (and understand), enjoy, and execute *thirds* and *sixths*, especially the former, in two-part song, which is the simplest and first used.

Thirds "begin and complete" all chords. With sixths, which are but inversions of thirds, they furnish most valuable practice, of which we can hardly have too much.   Dr. A. B. MARX.

TWO-PART SONG. BREAKING IN.

[BREAKING IN.—The Act of training, as of "breaking in" a horse.—WORCESTER.]

The teacher will explain how two parts are written on one staff: *First,* That when the measure or whole-rest is over the note it belongs to the upper part, as in the first measure; when it is below the note it belongs to the lower part; and that the quarter rest, as in the third measure belongs to both parts. *Second,* That the stems of the notes for the upper part point upward, and those for the lower part downward.

THIRDS.

SIXTHS, FIFTHS, AND THIRDS.

SUGGESTIONS TO TEACHERS.

Let the two exercises below (15 *a* and 15 *b*) be studied in the following order:

As to TIME.—*First*, Beat the time, naming the beats, commencing Up, Down, Left, Right, etc. *Second*, Beat the time, saying the Time-names instead of naming the beats. Be careful to whisper the rests.*

As to PITCH.—*First*, Say the scale-names without beating the time; *Second*, Say the pitch-names, without beating the time; *Third*, Sing the syllables, beating the time; *Fourth*, Never stop a class after they have commenced to sing an exercise or tune, *so long as any one in the class is singing right*, though all the rest fail. Make corrections and give further explanations after the courageous pupil has carried the exercise through.

If any of the pupils, especially the boys, find it difficult to reach the high notes, they may cease to sing them. It will be much to their credit if they can stop singing when the sounds are too high, and come in when the notes fall within the pitch of their voices.

The following song has both the above exercises on one staff, with words.

---

* A great deal has been said as to the doubtful utility of beating time with the hand. A careless manner of beating time is as bad as a clock out of order, or so imperfectly constructed that it "does not keep good time," and is worse than useless. Beating time should be according to a method, strictly adhered to: the motions should be uniform, that is, all the class should be *trained* to make the movements of the hands alike, and with the utmost precision.

THE RISING SUN.

1. Ar-rayed in gor-geous splen-dor, The beauteous, gold-en sun
2. We bid thee heart-y wel-come, Bright im-age of our God!

Be-gins with dawning glo-ry His dai-ly course to run.
Whose rays sublime and glo-rious Are pour-ing all a-broad.

3 How freshly doth all nature
  To life and beauty spring!
See how the glist'ning dew-drop
  To each green leaf doth cling?

4 How good is our Creator,
  Who made this shining light!
Come, brothers, to his praises
  Let us in song unite!

16 a.

16 b.

AWAKING SONG.

[May be transposed to Key of B-flat.]   Scholinua.

1. Re-fresh'd by gen - tle slumbers, From care and sor - row free,

Our hearts in tune - ful num-bers Sing praise, O Lord, to Thee.

2 Thou spreadest joy and blessing,
   Thou Source ot ev'ry good;
Then hear us, Thee addressing
   In songs of gratitude.

3 Oh, may we, ceasing never,
   Extol Thee all our days ;
Our hearts and life be ever
   An endless song of praise.

EXERCISES FOR TWO DIVISIONS ON ONE STAFF.

17.

18.

19 a.

19 b.

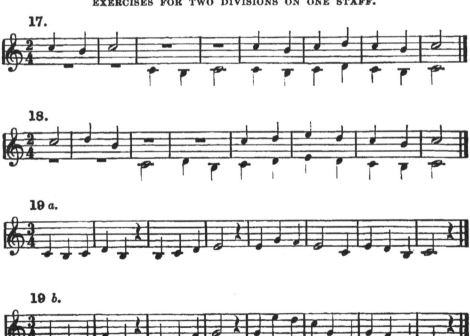

MORNING AWAKETH.

(May be transposed to B-flat.)

Dr. Marx.

1. Morn - ing a - wak - eth, Dark - ness is gone,
2. Birds with their mu - sic Fill the pure air;

In the bright heav - ens shin - eth the sun.
Flow - ers their fra - grance Breathe ev - 'ry - where.

3 Brightly the dew-drops
  Shine on the grass;
  Bees through the meadows
  Hum as they pass.

4 All is so joyful,
  All is so blest,
  Calmness and pleasure
  Fill ev'ry breast.

20 a.

20 b.

SPRING MORNING.

1. See how the fields are waking,   As   if from balm-y   sleep!
2. The fields in robes of flowers,   Smile back up - on the skies;

See! hill and dale are tak-ing   A green more bright and deep.
From all their blooming bowers,   Sweet clouds of in-cense rise.

3 The birds, in Spring rejoicing,   Sends from its hidden bosom
   Soar high in ether clear,   An off'ring, Lord, to thee.
   And warble many an anthem
   Ne'er meant for mortal ear.   5 All good from thee o'erflowing
                            On each created thing,
4 And many a desert blossom,   Life, light, and joy bestowing,
   Which eye will never see,   Returns to thee, its Spring.

Pursue the same method in teaching two-part songs, viz.,— *First,* Let all the class sing the second or lower part, and then the first, or upper part, as though there were no words; *Second,* When they know both parts, apply the words.

SUNDAY SONG.

21.

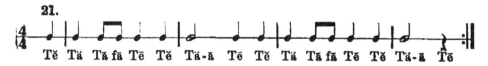

Tĕ   Tä   Tä fä Tē   Tĕ   Tä-ä   Tē   Tĕ   Tä   Tä fä Tĕ   Tŏ   Tä-ä   Tē

mf   H. G. NAGELI.

1. To - day   a   sol-emn still - ness Is rest - ing   far and near;
2. The Sab - bath bells are ring - ing, So cheer-ful   and   so   clear,

And so may we, with glad - ness, God's ho - ly day re - vere.
The call to pray'r and sing - ing, And God's good word to hear.

3 Who would not heed the message
   God sends us from above?
Who would not seek his blessing,
   His mercy, and his love?

4 And as the Eastern sages
   Were guided by a star,

So faith will lead us heav'nward,
   Where God and angels are.

5 Once with our heav'nly Father,
   No griefs to us can come;
We'll dwell in peaceful pleasures
   In that eternal home.

OUR FATHER.

H. G. NAGELI.

1. He who gave the star - light, Glit - ter - ing soft

moon - light, And the bless - ed sun - light,— He

help - eth and watch - eth both thee and me.

2 He who guides the river,
   Gliding onward ever,
   Never asking whither,—
He watcheth and guideth both thee and me.

3 He who made the flowers,
   Hills and woods and bowers,
   Tempests, clouds and showers,—
He helpeth and watcheth both thee and me.

PART II.—THE CHROMATIC SCALE.

LEARNING MORE ABOUT THE SCALE.

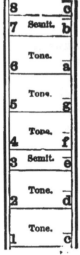

1. There are eight sounds in the scale.

2. They are named One, Two, Three, Four, Five, Six, Seven, Eight, represented by the figures 1, 2, 3, 4, 5, 6, 7, 8.

3. These eight sounds differ in pitch.

4. By pitch is meant the rising and falling of the voice, as in singing, step by step, up or down the scale.

5. The difference of pitch between two sounds of the scale, as between One and Two, Two and Three, Three and Four, etc., is called an Interval.

6. There are two kinds of intervals in the scale, large and small.

7. The large intervals are called Tones,

8. The small intervals are called Semitones.

9. The scale is used to measure the difference of pitch between sounds, as a yard-stick is used to measure cloth and the like.

All the exercises and songs thus far have been in the key of C.* By that is meant that the pitch of One has always been c. We are now to study exercises and songs in other keys.

When the scale is based on any other pitch than that of c, it requires the introduction of one or more sounds not found in the "natural" scale. These extra sounds are found in what is called the Chromatic Scale,

---

* I do not sympathize with those who entertain so much anxiety about becoming too familiar with the key of C. There are other difficulties than those of tune to be encountered and overcome. After the pupils have mastered the scale so as to read readily in the key of C, let them in that key wrestle with some of the hard things in *time*.

The "ox" and the "ass" may become so much accustomed to persons and places as to be unhappy in consequence of any change; but I find no difficulty with children nine years of age, in changing the places as to the pitch of the scale. After they have become familiar with one place, they are quite curious to know others. All the difficulties that have been overcome in one key, as to tune and time, are under our feet forever in all the others.

That good old rule, "Learn to do some one thing well, and every thing else by that," is especially to be applied in the art of reading music from the staff, in various keys.

which is made up of *First,* the eight sounds of the natural scale, which you have already learned, and *Second,* others, coming between such sounds of the natural scale as form intervals of a tone.

THE CHROMATIC SCALE ASCENDING.

8	c	Do
7	b	Si
♯6	a or ais	Li
6	a	La
♯5	g or gis	Si
5	g	Sol
♯4	f or fis	Fi
4	f	Fa
3	e	Mi
♯2	d or dis	Ri
2	d	Re
♯1	c or cis	Di
1	c	Do

You see by the diagram that there are five new sounds — just as many as there are large intervals or tones in the scale. You will observe that the new sounds have this sign (♯) called a Sharp, before each of them. It always indicates a sound one semitone higher than that named by the letter alone.

According to the diagram, the scale-names of the chromatic scale, commencing with c, are : One, Sharp-One, Two, Sharp-Two, Three, Four, Sharp-Four, Five, Sharp-Five, Six, Sharp-Six, Seven, Eight. When we say the pitch-names, the letters are called first, as *c*-sharp, *d*-sharp, *f*-sharp, *g*-sharp, and *a*-sharp.

The best way to hear how the chromatic scale sounds is to strike c̄, upon the piano, and then every key, white and black, up to c̿. A good cabinet organ will do as well, if not better.

The chromatic scale ascending appears on the staff thus :—

1.

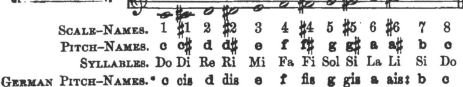

SCALE-NAMES.	1	♯1	2	♯2	3	4	♯4	5	♯5	6	♯6	7	8
PITCH-NAMES.	c	c♯	d	d♯	e	f	f♯	g	g♯	a	a♯	b	c
SYLLABLES.	Do	Di	Re	Ri	Mi	Fa	Fi	Sol	Si	La	Li	Si	Do
GERMAN PITCH-NAMES.*	c	cis	d	dis	e	f	fis	g	gis	a	ais‡	b	c

The chromatic scale is not to be sung as above, but as follows :—

---

* The German chromatic pitch-names are more convenient to sing than the English, because they can be said with one syllable. Dr. A. B. MARX, a great German writer on the teaching of singing, says that the difference of pitch is very much clearer in the mind when we say c, cis, than when we say c, c-sharp; and so of the other chromatic sounds.

with *g* hard as in *give.* ‡ Pronounced *ice.*

For Dicta-tion.	8	7	8	2	♯1	2	3	♯2	3	4
To be Sung.	Do	Si	Do	Re	Di	Re	Mi	Ri	Mi	Fa
	c	b	c	d	cis	d	e	dis	e	f

	5	♯4	5	6	♯5	6	7	♯6	7	8
	Sol	Fi	Sol	La	Si	La	Si	Li	Si	Do
	g	fis	g	a	gis	a	b	ais	b	c

Although any of the above chromatic sounds may appear in easy music, sharp-four is most frequently used, as in the following exercise.

SHARP–FOUR.

MORNING SONG.

1. Morning's golden light is breaking; Tints of beauty paint the skies;

Morning's feather'd choir are wak-ing, Bid-ding me from sleep a - rise.

2 Well, I'm ready; quiet resting
  Has restored my weary pow'rs;
I'll again, all sloth resisting,
  Labor thro' the day's bright hours.

3 But with thanks let me remember
  Him who gave me quiet sleep;
Let me all his mercies number,
  And his precepts gladly keep.

4 When I leave the downy pillow,
  Which so oft has borne my head,
Sure it's right a time to hallow
  To the Hand that kept my bed.

5 Let me never prove ungrateful,
  Let me never thankless be;
From a sin so base and hateful
  May I be for ever free!

THE CHROMATIC SCALE DESCENDING.

When we name a chromatic from the upper of the two sounds between which it occurs, we use the word *flat,* meaning a semitone *lower* than the natural sound from which it is named; so the sign which means a semitone lower is called a flat, and is made thus : ♭.

The chromatic scale descending, in which the intermediate or chromatic sounds are represented by flats, appears upon the staff thus:

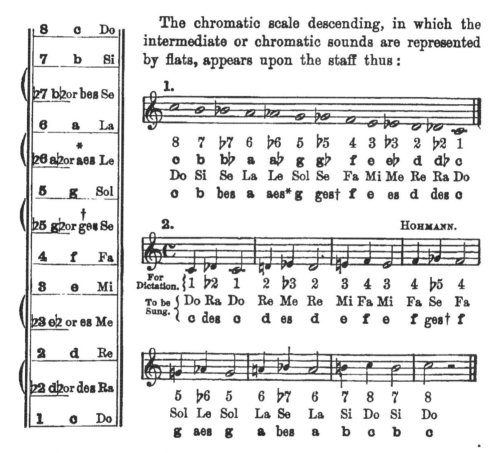

We have spoken of the first regular sounds of the scale being called *natural,* and of the intermediate sounds, *chromatic.* Besides the characters which are called *sharp* and *flat* (♯ and ♭), we have a character called a *natural,* (made thus, ♮), which is used to take away the effect of either the sharp or the flat.

Among the flat sounds that occur in singing, as chromatics, *flat-seven* will be met with most frequently.

---

* Pronounced *ace.*   † Pronounced with *g* hard, as in *get.*

FLAT—SEVEN.

ACCIDENTALS.

When sharps and flats appear in exercises and songs,—as in the second measure of Exercise 3 and the fourth measure of "Morning Song," page 46, and in the exercise with flat-seven,— they are called Accidentals.

"Songs are more numerous with accidental sharps and flats than without them; the singer must therefore make himself acquainted with the use of these characters."

The pupils need not be afraid of these accidental notes; they will be just as easy to sing as the scale itself. The flat-seven will require a little more *thinking* at first than sharp-four, as in the following song.

BEGINNING OF SPRING.

1. The Spring a - gain ap - pear - eth, The Spring our hearts that

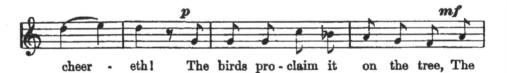

cheer - eth! The birds pro - claim it on the tree, The

scent-ed flow-ers tell it thee! The Spring again ap - pear - eth!

2 Ye see it in the meadows,
  And 'mid the forest's shadows;
  The cuckoo calls, the linnet sings,
  And with delight all nature rings,
  For Spring again appeareth!

3 Here buds their heads are raising,
  Here peaceful flocks are grazing;
  Ah! see how ev'ry heart is glad,
  How Earth is in her beauty clad,
  For Spring again appeareth!

EXERCISES IN CHROMATIC SOUNDS.

FIRST STEP.—The pupils should be able to sing at sight the following exercise, without hesitation or making a mistake.

SECOND STEP.—The second and third measures in the following
exercise will be found to be just as easy to sing as the first and fourth
measures.   The pupils should beat the time.

THIRD STEP.—The same exercise with the second part of each
measure left out.   The pupils should think of the sounds left out.

FOURTH STEP.—In Exercise No. 4, the teacher is to decide how
much to assist the pupils.

The teacher will explain the use of the natural (♮) in the last section.

FIFTH STEP.—If the previous exercise is well mastered, the following will be easy to sing.

---

* The question-mark indicates that there is something special to think about.

The following is a similiar exercise in three-four time.

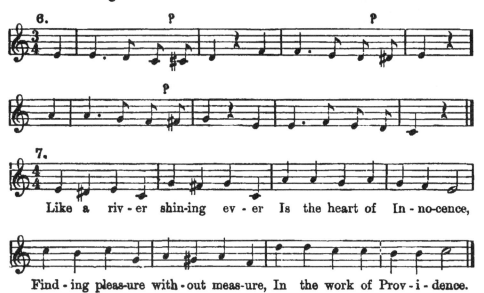

Like a riv - er shin-ing ev - er Is the heart of In - no-cence,

Find - ing pleas-ure with - out meas-ure, In the work of Prov - i - dence.

The *time* in the following exercise should be thoroughly mastered.

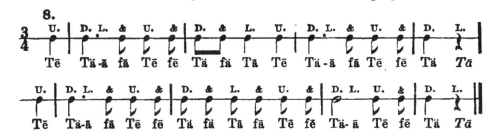

FLAT–SEVEN AND SHARP–ONE.

The two following exercises should be studied with great care, beating the time.

FAITH, LOVE AND HOPE.

1. Tho' Faith de-spair and wa - ver, A day of joy draws near, Our

home-ward path to cheer With light that shineth ev · · er.

2 Tho' Love may meet with sorrow,
  Yet should it not repine,
  A morning star shall shine
To greet us on the morrow.

3 Tho' Hope with fear be shaken,
  And all in darkness lie,
  A morning draweth nigh,
The sleeping to awaken.

KEY OF G.

By the Key is meant the pitch of *one* of the scale.

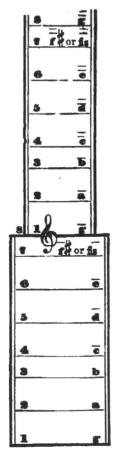

[The teacher will place Chart No. 25 before the class, and lead the pupils, somewhat as follows, to observe that the only difference between the key of G and the key of C is in the pitch.]

Teacher. The diagram represents two scales, one above the other. What is the pitch of *one* of the upper scale?

Pupils. Once-marked g.

T. [Gives the pitch $\bar{g}$, and dictates:] Sing the scale-names of the upper scale up and down.

Sing the syllables.

Sing the pitch-names.

What is the pitch of *eight* of the lower scale?

Sing the lower scale, descending and ascending, by the scale-names; by the syllables; by the pitch-names.

T. What chromatic sound do we find in this key?

P. F-sharp or fis.

T. Upon which degree?

P. Upon the seventh degree.

T. Why is f-sharp used instead of f?

P. To make the intervals right between six and seven, and between seven and eight.

The diagram appears upon the staff; thus:—

1.

The teacher will explain that as f-sharp or fis is peculiar to this key, it is placed upon the fifth line of the staff, just after the clef, as its signature or sign, and answers for the lower scale also.

The scales, as they have been sung from dictation, appear on the staff, with the signature, as follows:—

2.

1	2	3	4	5	6	7	8	8	7	6	5	4	3	2	1
g	a	b	c	d	e	fis	g	g	fis	e	d	c	b	a	g

3.

8	7	6	5	4	3	2	1	1	2	3	4	5	6	7	8
g	fis	e	d	c	b	a	g	g	a	b	c	d	e	fis	g

4.

1 2 3 4 5 6 5 6 5 4 3 2 2 1

5.

8 7 6 5 4 4 3 3 3 4 5 6 7 8

6.*

7.*

* Nos. 6 and 7 may be sung together.

8.

9.

THE LAMBKIN.

1. In the grass-y   plac - es, Where the flow'rs are seen,
2. On the sun - ny past - ure, Mer - ri - ly she springs;

There the lamb-kin graz - es,   On the ten - der green.
Feels, like us, the pleas - ure   Sun - ny Springtime brings.

3 Where the birds are blinking,   4 Softly there she rests her,
   To the brook she goes;   By the running stream;
When she's done her drinking,   We will not molest her,—
   Then she seeks repose.   Sweetly let her dream.

10.

11.

A, A, A.

1. A,   a,   a!   Now comes the mer-ry May;   Gone is   all   the
2. E,   e,   e!   A hap-py band are we,   Af-ter   A-pril's

win-try weath-er; Spring and blos-soms, come to-geth-er.
gen-tle show-ers, Comes sweet May, with fra-grant flow-ers.

A,   a,   a!   Now   comes   the   mer-ry   May.
E,   e,   e!   A   hap-py   band   are   we.

3 I, i, i!   To snow we've said good-by;
From the school-room hopping, skipping,
Down the stair-way dancing, tripping,
    I, i, i!   To snow we bid good-by.

4 O, o, o!   Now merrily we go;
Violets in the fields are springing,
Birds so sweetly now are singing,
    O, o, o!   Now merrily we go.

5 U, u, u!   I know what we will do:
O'er the meadows lightly straying,
By the brooklet gaily playing,
    U, u, u!   I know what we will do.

COMMENCING AFTER UP-BEAT, OR ON få.

THE BEAUTIFUL WORLD.

C. H. HOHMANN.

1. How love-ly   is this world! Here man - y joys to   us are giv'n,
2. It   is   no vale of tears! For God hath made it pass-ing fair,

Bless-ings fall   on   us all; How love-ly   is   this world!
Good and fair, pass-ing fair; This is   no   vale of tears!

3 The fields in green array'd, The cheerful sunshine warm and bright,
For our joy, for our joy, Our great Creator made.

4 He made the fountain, too; The field, that gives us daily bread,
  He did make for our sake,— Our God so good and true.

5 He gave us parents good, Who, that we may good children be,
  And may thrive, ever strive! He gave them for our good.

6 God made these for our sake! Then, whether rain or sunshine be,
  Courage take, for his sake! O children, courage take!

GOD THE LORD.

2 Canst thou count the insects playing
    In the sunshine's glowing light?
  Canst thou count the fishes straying
    In the sparkling waters bright?
  God the Lord a name has given .
    To all creatures under heaven,
  |: When he called them into life. :|

3 Canst thou count the children daily
    Rising from their beds at morn,—
  Going forth to wander gaily,
    By no care or trouble worn?
  God the Lord in all delighteth,
    And their goodness he requiteth;
  |: Thee, too, he doth know and love. :|

SPRING WANDERING SONG.

1. Birds are sing - ing, flow-ers bloom-ing, Nat-ure smil-ing, ev - 'ry -
2. Like the bird in cage im - pris-on'd, Have we been the win - ter

where; Let us forth with - out de - lay - ing, O'er the
through; Now the cage is o - pen'd for us, Win - ter

pleas - ant mead-ows stray-ing, Thro' the wood so green and fair.
hangs no long - er o'er us, Let us fly, then, forth a - new.

3 Joy reigns thro' reviving nature,   4 Let us all then freely wander
   Round us, with us, where we throng;   O'er the hill and verdant plain,
Joy is murm'ring in the bow'rs,   Thro' the fields and sunny meadows,
   Breathes from out the fragrant flowers   'Mid the woods refreshing shadows,
From the nightingale's glad song.   Forth into the world again.

EXERCISES IN TWO—FOUR TIME.

[*Always beat the time.* Teacher and pupils alternately, speaking the time names very distinctly.]

15.

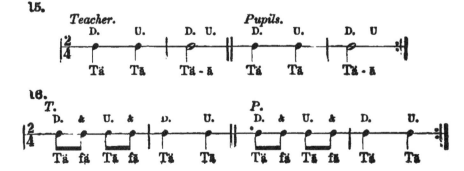

16.

FOUR SOUNDS IN EACH PART OF THE MEASURE FOR THE FIRST TIME.
[NOT DIFFICULT.]

When there are four sounds of equal length in each part of the measure in double time, the time-names are Tä zä fä nä, Tä zä fä nä.

17.

These three exercises should be copied upon the blackboard at first, unless the pupils are well accustomed to using books.

In beating time, the motion should be from the wrist only, and the hand should move very quickly, without making the least noise.

THE DOTTED QUARTER-NOTE IN TWO-FOUR TIME.

18.

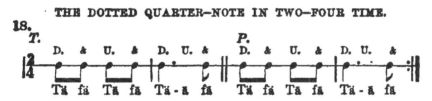

It will greatly assist the mind in comprehending the relative value of the dotted quarter-note, to think of it as *two beats long*. Both the down- and up-beats are perfectly performed, and the hand is at rest after making the up-beat, before the eighth-note which follows is sung.

THE DOTTED EIGHTH-NOTE.—[NOT DIFFICULT.]

19.

The above exercises should be done with spirit, both as to beating time and uttering the time-names. Right practice only, will secure a clear understanding of the dotted eighth-note. It may be well to repeat each of the above exercises four times.

PRAISE OF SINGING.

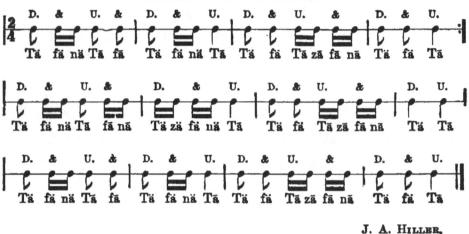

D. & U. & D. & U. D. & U. & D. & U.

Tä fä nä Tä fä Tä fä nä Tä Tä fä Tä zä fä nä Tä fä Tä

D. & U. & D. & U. D. & U. & D. U.

Tä fä nä Tä fä nä Tä zä fä nä Tä Tä fä Tä zä fä nä Tä Tä

D. & U. & D. & U. D. & U. & D. & U.

Tä fä nä Tä fä Tä fä nä Tä Tä fä Tä zä fä nä Tä fä Tä

J. A. HILLER.

ALLEGRO.

1. { Chil - dren all with cheer-ful - ness Let your songs be ring - ing! }
   { Mu - sic all your lives will bless, Therefore still be sing-ing! }

Sing-ing smooths the rug - ged way Thro' this vale of sor - row;

Sing - ing cheers the dark-est day, Brings the bright-est mor - row.

2 When good humor flies away,
　　Then come care and sadness;
　Quickly sing a cheerful lay,—
　　All will soon be gladness;
　Music cheers the darkest hours,
　　Peace and comfort bringing;
　What the dew is to the flow'rs,
　　To the soul is singing.

3 Sing the larks in yonder sky,
　　Sing the birds at even,
　Swallows from the house-top cry,—
　　All give thanks to Heaven.
　Forest, field, and meadow too,
　　With their songs are ringing;
　Wherefore, children, should not you
　　Evermore be singing?

THE SILV'RY MOON ADVANCES.

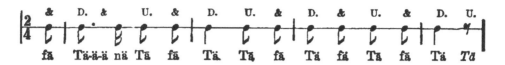

fä Tä-ä-ä nä Tä fä Tä Tä fä Tä fä Tä fä Tä Tä

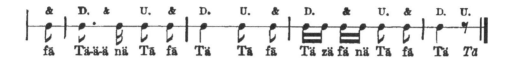

fä Tä-ä-ä nä Tä fä Tä Tä fä Tä zä fä nä Tä fä Tä Tä

1. The sil - v'ry moon ad - van - ces, O'er lof - ty hill and tree,
2. She comes, so soft - ly steal - ing, A - cross the stil - ly night;

Who, 'mid the star - ry dan - ces, So beau - ti - ful as she?
How man - y hearts are hail - ing, Her mild and friend - ly light!

3 Our eyes she gently closes,
    When daily toil is o'er;
The weary earth reposes
    Beneath her soothing power.

4 She comes with night-dews, healing
    The soul with pain distress'd;
She wakes the sweetest feeling
    Within the lonely breast.

5 Our heavenly Father lends us
    This trusty friend by night;
May he a spirit send us,
    As pure as her pure light.

SOME OF THE MOST COMMON CHROMATIC SOUNDS IN THE KEY OF G.

SHARP—FOUR IN THE LOWER SCALE.

THE EVENTIDE.

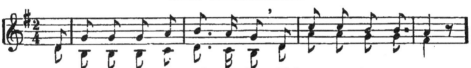

1. Oh! lay your wea - ry work a - side Oh! put your cares a - way;
2. How sweet when work is laid a - side, And closed the doors of school,

It is the plea-sant e - ven-tide, The mer - ry time of play.
A-mong the spread-ing trees to hide, That shade the lim - pid pool;

And hark! the shout-ing on the green, And by the pal - ing grey,
Let joy, then light up ev - 'ry face, Come all, with glad ar - ray,

Where man-y a mer - ry face is seen, As gen - tly falls the day.
And let us run a mer - ry race, As gen - tly falls the day.

[3rd stanza at foot of opposite page.]

Oh, wake and let your songs resound, And let your songs re - sound,

For sa - cred free-dom here is found, For free-dom here is found.

TRUTH AND HONESTY.

From the German, by Mrs. SHINDLER.   W. A. MOZART.

1. Let pre-cious truth and hon-es - ty At - tend thee all thy days,
2. Then, as on past-ures fair and green Thro' life thy feet shall roam,

And turn not thou a fin-ger's breadth From God's most holy ways.
Nor fear nor ter - ror shalt thou feel, When death shall call thee home.

3 The wicked man in all he does
  Is ever sore distressed;
  His vices drive him to and fro;
  His soul can find no rest.

4 The joyous Spring, the waving trees,
  For him smile all in vain;
  His soul is bent on lies and fraud,
  And on ill-gotten gain.

5 To him the leaf by breezes stirred
  Has terror in its sound;
  And when he 's buried in the grave,
  His soul no rest has found.

6 Then practise truth and honesty
  Through all thine earthly days,
  And turn not thou a finger's breadth
  From God's most holy ways.

[Concluded from opposite page.]

3 Oh! pleasant is the merry ring,
  The race o'er hill and dale,
  And lightsome are the hearts that sing,
  When ev'ning sports prevail.

But fainter, fainter grows the sound,
  Less jocund is the play, [round
  For twilight shades are gath'ring
  As gently falls the day.

KEY OF D.

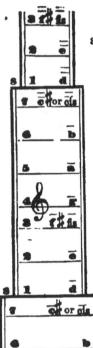

[Chart No. 27 is placed before the class.   Questions to be answered from the diagram.]

What is the pitch of *one* in this key?
What is the pitch of *three?* Of *seven?*
Which sound of the scale comes with the g-clef?
What new chromatic sound in this key?
Why is c-sharp or cis used in this key?
Why is f-sharp or fis used in this key?

[The teacher will lead the class to know how to get the pitch d̄ from the pitch-pipe, (either from c̄ or ḡ), and have the pupils sing the middle scale by the scale-names, syllables, and pitch-names; then the upper and lower scales. The teacher may write, in figures, some well known tune upon the black board, as follows, and have the scholars sing it.]

1.
D.$\frac{4}{4}$ 3– 3, 2,|3, 5, 5–|3– 3, 2,|1– 0–:|8–8, 6,|
    6, 5, 5–|3, 2, 3, 5,|6, 5, 5–|8– 8, 6,|6, 5, 5–|
    3– 3, 2,|1– 0–‖

The diagram appears upon the staff thus:—

2.

[The teacher will explain the key signature, write it upon the blackboard, and have the pupils copy it; thus:

It should not be any longer neccessary to write the parts separately for the convenience of study. In all two-part songs, let the second or lower part be learned first, by all the class; then the first or upper part. All the songs should be learned by *note*, both as to time and tune; just as if there were no words to the music.]

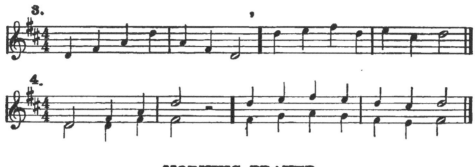

3.

4.

MORNING PRAYER.

1. To   Thee,   Fa - ther,   Cheer - ful thanks I   pay;
2. Sweet - est   slum - ber,   Night has giv - en   me;

Thou   hast   brought me   To an - oth - er   day.
Sleep   re - fresh - ing, Makes me strong to   be.

3 This day, dawning,
  Bringeth new delight
Let me, Father,
  Spend it, then, aright.

4 Heavenly Father,
  Oh! thy blessing give;
That obedient
  I may ever live!

Exercises Nos. 2 and 3, upon Chart 27, are not so difficult in the time as they appear to be. This is a good opportunity for mastering the dotted eighth followed by a sixteenth, in four-four time, as in the second measure of No. 2. If the pupils meet with any difficulty in comprehending these time relations, the following exercises may help them to put the enemy under their feet.

TIME EXERCISES IN FOUR—FOUR MEASURE.

5.

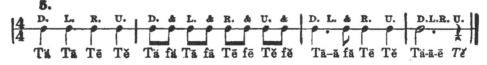

FOUR SOUNDS OF EQUAL LENGTH IN EACH PART OF A FOUR–FOUR MEASURE.

(First time, by the teacher; second time, by the pupils.)

6.

Tä zä fä nä Tä zä fä nä Tĕ zĕ fĕ nĕ Tĕ zĕ fĕ nĕ Tä Tä fä Tĕ Tĕ

THE DOTTED EIGHTH–NOTE.

(First time, by the teacher; second time, by the pupils.)

7.

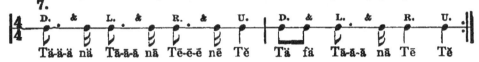

Tä-ä-ä nä Tä-ä-ä nä Tĕ-ĕ-ĕ nĕ Tĕ Tä fä Tä-ä-ä nä Tĕ Tĕ

SOME OF THE MOST USUAL CHROMATIC SOUNDS IN THE KEY OF D.

8.

8	7	8	2	#1	2	3	#2	3	4
d	cis	d	e	dis	e	fis	eis*	fis	g

5	#4	5	6	#5	6	7	#6	7	8
a	gis	a	b	ais	b	cis	bis	cis	d

9.

Tĕ fĕ Tä-ä fä Tĕ Tĕ Tä-ä-ä nä Tä-ä-ä nä Tĕ Tĕ Tä-ä-ĕ Tĕ Tä-ä Tĕ

10.

---

* Pronounced *ees.*

EVENING SONG.

1. If I've ful-filled my dai - ly task a-right, And

ev - 'ry du - ty done, Then joy to me when

dark - est shades of night Shall cloud the sink - ing

sun; How cheer - ing, then, how calm - ing, The

gold - en lin - g'ring ray! The ev - en - tide is

charm - - - - ing That ends a well - spent day.

2 But woe to him whose eye that hour is dim
    With sin-repenting tears;
No anguish ever can restore to him
    The joys of wasted years.
Oh, precious are the power
    And time that God has giv'n:
May I each passing hour
    Lay up some store in heaven!

FOUR SOUNDS OF EQUAL LENGTH IN EACH PART OF A THREE-FOUR MEASURE.

(First time, the teacher; second time, the pupils.)

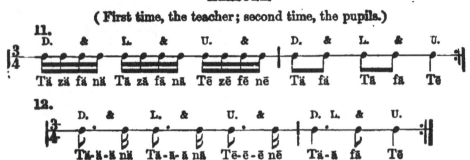

THE FLOW'RET.

1. A-lone I wan-der'd in for-est wild, With care-less footsteps the time be-guil'd, With careless footsteps the time be-guil'd.

2 A tiny flow'ret was blooming there,
|: Like eyes it sparkled; t'was starlike fair. :|

8 I stooped to break it, and heard it say:
|: "Wilt thou, then, break me to fade away? :|

4 I plucked it gently, both root and flow'r,
|: Homeward I bore it unto my bow'r, :|

5 Again to plant it in shelter there;
|: And still it blossoms, that flow'ret fair. :|

THE MOON.

MODERATO.   J, MERLING.

1. Love - ly moon, that soft - ly glides Through the

realms where God a - bides; Through the realms of

up - per sky, In the arch - ed heav'ns on high;—

2 In the gloomy night, thy ray
Lights the pilgrim on his way:
When the shades of darkness come,
Thou dost guide him to his home.

3 Bright thy smile when cares annoy,
Token of that heav'nly joy
That shall reign in realms above,
Breaking forth in songs of love.

THE CALL TO PRAYER.

Be - hold how brightly morn-ing A - wakes each bird and flow'r, The

hills and lakes a - dorn - ing, While church bell's solemn warn-ing Pro -

claims pray'r's sa - cred hour, Pro - claims pray'r's sa - cred hour.

KEY OF A.

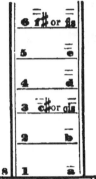

The pupils will observe by looking at the diagram, that in the lower scale there are three chromatic sounds, and that the new one, g-sharp or gis, comes upon the seventh degree of the scale.

Instead of writing the g-sharp on the second line, after the f-sharp and c-sharp, thus:

It is written upon the first space above the staff, thus:

[The teacher will practise from Chart 29, as in the previous keys; also, the following, by the syllables and pitch-names. Notice carefully that the long notes at the end of a phrase are given their full time.]

FLAT—SEVEN IN THE KEY OF A.

1   3   5   8   8   ♭7   6   5   4   5   1
a cis e   a   a   g fis e   d   e   a

6.

SHARP—FOUR IN THE KEY OF A.

7.

5   8   7   6   5   ♯4 5   5   3   4   5   6   7   8
e   a gis fis e dis e   e cis d   e fis gis a

8.

INDEPENDENCE-DAY.

1. This day   to greet, With joy we meet; Then ban - ish care   a -
2. Our fa - thers brave, The land to save, Did free-dom's call   o -

way!   With   fes - tive cheer, Come, has - ten here; 'T is
bey!   By   young and old Their deeds   be   told; 'T is

In - de - pen-dence - Day,   'T is In - de - pen-dence - Day!

COME AND SEE HOW HAPPILY.

English Air.

1. Come and see how hap-pi-ly We spend the day,

Al-ways join-ing cheer-ful-ly In school or play;

In our books and sports combined, Man-y are the joys we find.

2 We improve the present hour,   But with study and with song,
   For swift it flies;   Time with us still glides along.
Youth is but a passing flow'r,   Come and see how happily
   Which blooms and dies;   We spend the day, etc.

CHILDHOOD.

1. { O time of sim-ple pleas-ures! I nev-er can for-get }
   { Those hap-py hours of child-hood, Like peace-ful jew-els set; }

I sleep with-out a sor-row, And wake with ear-ly morn,

To watch the sun-ny mor-row Rise thro' the ro-sy dawn.

2 No cares or griefs distress me,   I strive to please my teachers
   The future is all bright;   By diligence and love,
In parents, brothers, sisters,   And day by day endeavor
   I constantly delight;   My gratitude to prove.

FRIENDSHIP.

1. A - wake, a - wake the tune - ful voice, And strike the joy - ful
2. 'T is not the cold and for - mal drawl That wakes the in - ward

strings; We 'll pour the mel - low notes a - long, And
flame: But 't is the song that glows like fire, The

raise a peal-ing, gladd'n-ing song, Till heav'n with mu-sic rings.
song that feel-ing hearts in - spire,—A mu - sic worth the name.

3 But hark! those sweet, concordant notes,
    That breathe a magic spell,
    That seem like songs the angels sing,
    Like sounds which have in heav'n their spring,
    Where holy beings dwell,—

4 'T is these that glow from Friendship's soul;
    'T is these that speak the heart:
    'T is these that show the peaceful mind,
    The spirit meek and pure and kind,
    Unstained by vicious art.

5 Oh, yes! 't is here that music dwells,
    In Friendship's sweet abode;
    'T is here that notes concordant sound,
    'T is here that harmony is found
    Like that which dwells with God.

CHANGE OF SEASONS.

From the German, by Mrs. S. B. DANA SHINDLER.

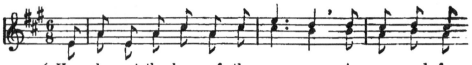

1. How pleas-ant the change of the sea-sons, As on-ward for
What pleas-ure, what joy nev-er-end-ing They bring to the

ev - er they roll!
care - wea - ried soul!

The Spring with its warmth and its

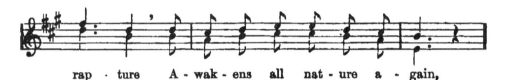

rap - ture A - wak - ens all nat - ure a - gain,

Gives life to the trees and the riv - ers, The

seeds and the mead - ows and plain.

2 The long shining day of the Summer
  Do ripen the birth of Spring,
And when we are weary, complaining,
  Do soft cooling fruits to us bring;
And then comes the wonderful blessing
  Which Autumn so richly doth yield,
When ripens the grass in the meadow,
  And ripens the grain in the field.

3 Then Winter comes, silently pouring
  Her white, fleecy snow on the ground;
Tho' cold and tho' stormy, what pleasure
  In skating and sleighing is found!
So love we the change of the seasons,
  As onward for ever they roll;
For pleasure and joy never-ending
  They bring to the care-wearied soul.

WISDOM OF YOUTH.

From the French.+
F. LAUTERBURG.

RATHER LIVELY.

1. Way-ward child, re - flect - ing nev - er, Pause to
   For the days pass on - ward ev - er, And no

pro - fit by the light; Ev - 'ry step wher - ev - er
pow'r can check their flight.

turn - ing, Ev - 'ry i - dle hour we spend, Ev - 'ry

tho't, and plaint, and yearn-ing, Near-er, near - er brings the end.

2	3
Moments flee, and all things teach us 　That the past comes ne'er again ; All too soon the time must reach us, 　When regrets shall be in vain. Let not glowing youth's fair treasures 　Fade in indolence away ; Know that life's enduring pleasures 　Grow from action, day by day.	Oh, remember thy Creator, 　While thy life's without a care ; So his grace shall guide thee later, 　Saving thee from sin and snare ; When thy head by age is whitened, 　Warning thee that death is near, All thy life by God's love brightened, 　Thou shalt go without a fear.

KEY OF E.

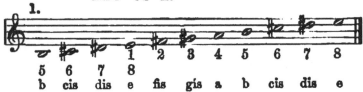

[The pupils should be directed to give their attention to the diagram on Chart 31 (or that on this page), and examined as to the pitch-names. They will observe that the new chromatic sound in the formation of the scale in this key is d-sharp (or, in singing, dis), and that it comes on the seventh degree. There will be no difficulty in going directly to the practice of the following exercises and songs. They should also be required to beat the time in these and all exercises, and care should be taken that this be done with precision and quietness. Beating time is of no avail unless well done. If the beating be sluggish, the singing will be of the same quality.

We have now had the scale and songs in five different keys, but have said nothing about the relation of one key to another. There are four more keys to be learned, making in all nine. The study of Modulation from one key to another is given its natural place in the Third Series of Charts and Third Reader, where it is presented from a harmonic point of view, in accordance with the best authorities.]

5.

6.

THE JOYS OF INNOCENCE.

Chorus.

1. Joy is round us, smil - ing ev - 'ry where!
2. Love is rul - ing, work - ing ev - 'ry where,

Duet.

On the hills and riv - ers smil - ing, Ev - 'ry hu - man
In the cool and sha - dy bow - ers, Where the trees are

Chorus.

care be - guil - ing; Joy is round us, smil - ing ev - 'ry where.
decked with flow-ers; Love is rul - ing, work - ing ev - 'ry where.

3 Pleasure echoes, echoes far and near,
From the green banks decked with flowers,
Sunny hills and pleasant bowers;
Pleasure echoes, echoes far and near.

4 Maiden, up, and weave a flow'ry crown:
See the buds their leaves unfolding;
Love her festival is holding:
Maiden, up, and weave a flow'ry crown.

5 Go ye forth and join the May-day throng;
Sings the cuckoo by the river;
In the breeze the young leaves quiver;
Go ye forth and join the May-day throng.

PEACE.

1. Gen - tle Peace, from heav'n de - scend - ed, We would
2. Thou hast thrown a smile of beau - ty O'er the

live be - neath thy law; Thou hast home and
mead - ow, hill, and grove; Thou hast quick - ened

life be - friend-ed, Nurse of no - bler deeds than war.
us to du - ty, Thou hast warmed our hearts to love.

3 Ours is now each smiling flower,
    Ours the lofty mountain-pine,
Ours the fruit-tree's golden shower,
    And the close-entwining vine.

4 Still stay with us, still replenish
    Fields with fruit, ourselves with love;
Discord and dissension banish,
    Peaceful Spirit from above.

CHILDHOOD PLEASURES.

ALLEGRO.

1. { Come, let us, sing - ing, speak out those pleas - ures;
   { We prize them high - ly, a - bove all treas - ures;

Which crown our child - hood, those days so dear;
How bright their sun - shine, how sweet, how clear!

Our days are May - days, with - out a cloud, Then let us,

sing - ing, re-joice a - loud. Our child-hood pleas-ures are like the

riv ers, Whose on-ward flow - ing is deep and free.

2 Oh, how we're favored, to live so cheerful,
    So free from sorrow and free from care,
While many round us are sad and tearful,
    For sad misfortune does not them spare;
Then we'll be happy while yet we can,
While days of childhood shall yet remain.
          Our childhood, etc.

3 Yes, we will ever, by night and daily,
    Sing forth our pleasures in full good cheer;
We're yet in childhood, and all goes gaily;
    Our age of sadness is not yet near;
Then let our voices rescund aloud;
For all is sunshine,—there's not a cloud.
          Our childhood, etc.

SHARP—FOUR IN E.

5 ♯4 5

HOW LOVELY, HOW CHARMING.

German.

LIVELY.

1. How love - ly, how charm-ing, has na - ture been made! The
2. How green are the mead-ows! how bright is the morn! How

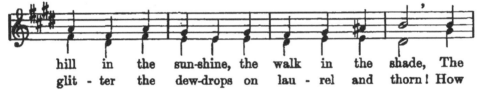

hill in the sun-shine, the walk in the shade, The
glit - ter the dew-drops on lau - rel and thorn! How

wild rose, a - dorn - ing the hedge with its bloom, And
pearl - y and pure is the bri - ar in bloom! How

load - ing the air with its wealth of per - fume!
love - ly the May-flow'rs, how sweet their per - fume!

3 The aspen-tree flutters, and whispers its fear;
   The linden invites all the bees to draw near;
   The willow bends low its frail branches to lave
   In the lake, where the clouds seem to float on the wave.

4 How lovely, how cheering, has nature been made!
   The flow'rs in the sunshine, the brook in the shade,—
   All, all with their charms, were bestowed with our birth,
   To cheer aud enliven our pathway on earth.

THE WANDERER'S RETURN.

Italian Melody.

1. When, my fa - ther's home for - sak - ing, Far o'er
2. When, in dis - tant lands a ran - ger, None I

sea and land to wan - der,—When, each tie that bound me
found to know and love me,—When, a lone and wea - ry

break - ing, Proud of free - dom, gay I roamed,— Sweet - ly
stran - ger, Sad, I pined for friends and home,— Then how

smiled the world be - fore me, Sweet - ly smiled the heav - en
sad the world be - fore me; Then how chill the heav'ns frown'd

o'er me, Hope on joy - ful pinions bore me Over paths with flow'rs bestrew'd.
o'er me, Hope no long-er gai - ly bore me, Flow'rs for me no longer bloom'd.

3 When my footsteps, homeward turning,
    Sought once more the household altar,—
When my heart, impatient burning,
    Long'd the dear ones there to greet,—
Then how smiled dear home before me!
Then sweet memory flutter'd o'er me,
Then sweet hope's light pinions bore me,
    Peace and joy at home to meet.

KEY OF F.

It will be observed that each new key; starting from the key of C, has been founded upon *Five* of the key before it: G was Five in the key of C; D was Five in the key of G; A was Five in the key of D; and E was Five the key of A.

In the keys with flats, starting from C, each new key is founded upon *Four* of the preceding key; thus, F is Four in the key of C, and the same relation will be observed in the succeeding keys with additional flats.

In this key, as may be seen by the diagram, it becomes necessary to use the chromatic sound b-flat (or, in singing, *bes*) to make the semitone come right between three and four of the scale.

The diagram appears on the staff, thus:

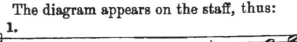

As b-flat (or bes) is the only chromatic sound in this key, its sign is placed on the third line of the staff as in the following exercises.

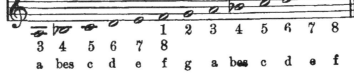

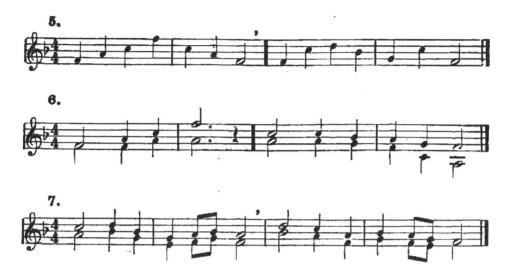

You will remember that on Chart 29, Ex. 4, *flat-seven* was produced by the use of a natural, (♮). In this key, *sharp-four,* is produced by means of a natural, as in the following example.

SOWING FLOWERS.

1.   Lit - tle seed, now must thou go   To thy still, cold bed be - low;
2. Couldst thou know what 'tis I   do,   And couldst tell thy sor-rows, too,

Do   as   thou   art   bid - den!   Now the earth must cov - er thee,
This were thy   com - plain - ing: "Ne'er shall I   the sun be - hold,

And no eye shall ev - er see Where thou li - est hid - den.
In this grave, so dark and cold! Ah, my life is wan - ing!"

3 But take courage, little seed;
   Though thou liest here, indeed,
      Gentle slumber taking,
   Yet thou'lt soon in upper air
   As a flower bloom so fair,
      To new life awaking!

4 I shall one day lie as thou
   In thy dark bed liest now,
      When death shall befall me;
   But in glory shall I rise
   To the realms above the skies,
      When the Lord doth call me.

COMMENCING AFTER THE UP-BEAT.

12.
FIRMLY.

A - rouse ye, a - rouse ye, And wel - come the dawn - ing.

NEVER SAY FAIL.

MODERATO. GLASER.

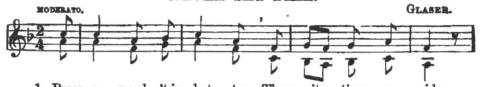

1. Press on - ward—'t is bet - ter Than sit - ting a - side,
2. With eye that is o - pen, A tongue that's not dumb,

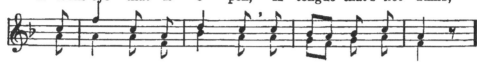

And dream - ing and sigh - ing, And wait - ing the tide;
And heart that will nev - er, To sor - row suc - cumb,

In life's ear - nest bat - tle, They on - ly pre - vail,
We 'll bat - tle and con - quer, Tho' thou - sands as - sail

Who dai - ly march on - ward, And nev - er say fail.
How strong and how might - y, Who nev - er say fail.

3 Then onward, right onward,
    And press on your way,
Unheeding the envious
    Who would you betray;
All obstacles vanish,
    All enemies quail,
In fear of their wisdom
    Who never say fail.

4 In life's rosy morning,
    In manhood's firm pride,
Let this be the motto
    Our footsteps to guide;
In storm and in sunshine,
    Whatever assail,
We 'll onward and conquer,
    And never say fail.

HOW LOVELY ARE THE WOODS.

1. How love - ly are the woods! The ver-dant, ver-dant woods!
2. Oh, how I love the woods! The ver-dant, ver-dant woods!

Where sweetly the birds are all sing-ing, And thanks for the morning are
Where light-ly the branch-es are twink-ling With drops of the dew that are

ring - ing, A - round in the ver - dant woods, The ver -dant, ver - dant
sprinkling The leaves of the ver - dant woods, The ver -dant, ver - dant

woods. Tra la la la la la la la la la la la, Tra la.

3 O come then to the woods!
  The verdant, verdant woods!
The echo that dwells by the mountain,
Will answer your voice by the fountain
  That springs in the verdant woods,
  The verdant, verdant woods.
    Tra la la, &c.

4 How lovely are the woods!
  The verdant, verdant woods!
Where sweetly the birds are all singing.
And thanks for the morning are ringing,
  Around in the verdant woods.
  The verdant, verdant woods.
    Tra la la, &c.

FLAT—SEVEN IN THE KEY OF F.

1	3	5	8	8	♭7	6	5	4	5	1
f	a	c	f	f	es	d	c	bes	c	f

The above will be recognized to be the same as Ex. 3, page 42.

In the following exercise, and in "The Hunter's Prize," the flat-seven occurs in the lower scale. It is not difficult to sing.

14.

5	3	5	8	♭7	6	5	4	4	3	3	5	4	3
Sol	Mi	Sol	Do	Se	La	Sol	Fa	Fa	Mi	Mi	Sol	Fa	Mi
c	a	c	f	es	d	c	bes	bes	a	a	c	bes	a

THE HUNTER'S PRIZE.

German.

ANDANTE.

1. A hun-ter, ear-ly rang-ing A-long the for-est wild,
2. Fair, queen-ly Faith come fore - most; Next, Love be-fore him passed,

Saw o'er the green-sward trip - ping, trip - - ping, Three
With Hope, all bright and smil - ing, smil - - ing, The

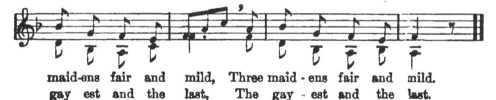

maid-ens fair and mild, Three maid-ens fair and mild.
gay est and the last, The gay - est and the last.

And said, "Now choose between us,
  For one with thee will stay :
Choose well, or thou may'st rue it, rue it,
  |: When two have passed away." :|

4 He said, "All bright and lovely,
  Oh, why must two depart ?
Faith, Hope, Love, stay together, together !
  |: Possess and share my heart !" :|

KEY OF B-FLAT.

It will be seen by the diagram that the new chromatic sound in the formation of the scale in this key, is e-flat (or, in singing, es), and comes on the fourth degree.

The diagram appears on the staff, thus:

THE CHINESE GOLDEN RULE.

Be to oth - ers kind and true, As you'd have them be to you;

Nev - er do nor say to men That which you'd not take a - gain.

(First time, the teacher; second time, the pupils.)

THROUGH THY PROTECTING CARE.

1. { Through thy pro - tect - ing care   Kept   till   the   morn - ing,
   { Taught to draw near in pray'r, Heed   we   the   warn - ing:
D. C.—Ev - er - more prais - ing thee, God   of   the   morn - ing.

Make bright our   way   to Thee; Glad - ly   our souls would   be

2 God of our sleeping hours, In us thy work fulfil;
 Watch o'er us waking,   Be with thy children still,
 All our imperfect powers Those who obey thy will
 In thy hands taking.   Never forsaking.

6.

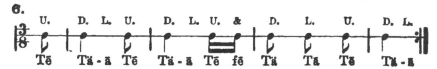

 U. D. L. U. D. L. U. &. D. L. U. D. L.
 Tē Tă - ă Tē Tă - ă Tē fē Tă Tă Tē Tă - ă

SWEET RURAL SCENE.

Dr. Young.   German.

1. Sweet ru - ral scene Of flocks and green! At   care   less
2. In   pros - pect wide, The bound - less tide! Waves cease   to

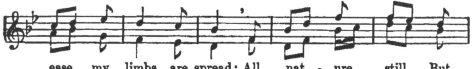

ease   my   limbs are spread; All   nat - ure   still, But
foam   and winds to   roar; With - out   a   breeze, The

yon - der   rill, And lis - t'ning pines nod o'er my head.
cur - ling seas Dance on   in   meas - ure to   the shore.

7.

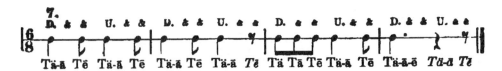

Tä-a Tē   Tä-a Tē   Tä-a Tē   Tä-a Tē   Tä Tä Tē   Tä-a Tē   Tä-ä-ē   Tä-a Tē

SHARP—ONE AND SHARP—SIX.

8.

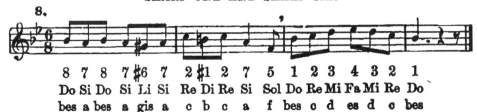

8   7   8   7 #6   7   2 #1   2   7   5   1   2   3   4   3   2   1

Do Si Do Si Li Si   Re Di Re Si Sol Do Re Mi Fa Mi Re Do

bes a bes a gis a   c b c a f bes c d es d c bes

PROVIDENCE.

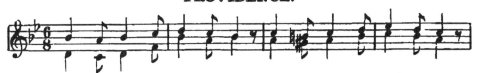

1. He   who made the stars on high   Rules su-preme o'er earth and sky;
2. He   who marks the spar-row's fall   Looks with ten - der - ness on all;

Here   we   all   our   hom-age bring, And grate-ful prais - es   sing.
Him   we   trust our souls   to keep; His mer - cy   can - not sleep.

3 Though our life is but a span,
    Endless is the soul of man,
    May we all, then, look above,
    And trust a God of love.

SHARP—FIVE.

9.

1   2   3   4   6 #5   5   6   4   3   5   8   6 #5   5   6   4   3   1

Do   Re Mi Fa   La Si La Fa Mi Sol Do   La Si La Fa Mi   Do

bes   c   d   es   g fis g es d f bes   g fis g es d   bes

FIRST DAYS OF SPRING.

From the French. +

J. GREITH.

ALLEGRETTO.

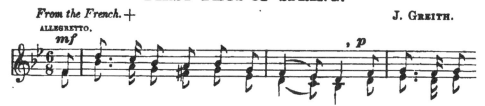

1. The   fields are now blooming with   flow - ers; How charming and
2. Each   leaf - let and bud, green and   ten - der, Pro-claims the good

love - ly   the   sight!   The   sun   and the   soft   A - pril
hand   of   the   Lord;   The   tune - ful birds prais - es   all

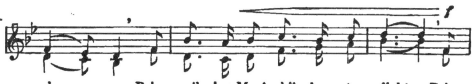

show - ers Bring smil - ing May's chil -dren   to   light,   Bring
ren - der To   him who cre - ates   by   his   word,   To

smil - ing May's chil - dren   to   light.
him   who   cre - ates   by   his   word.

3 The apple-tree buds, faintly blushing,
   Perfume the clear air all around;
   The long-prisoned brook, gladly rushing,
   |: Leaps onward with musical sound. :|

4 All Nature lifts myriad voices,
   That sound the whole forest along;
   The bird and the flower rejoices,—
   |: Come, join we the jubilant throng! :|

TRAVELLING.

1. To wan - der is the mil - ler's joy! What kind of mil - ler
2. From wa - ter we have learned it;—yes, It knows no rest by

can he be, Who ne'er hath learn'd to wan-der free, To wan - der,
night or day, But wan-ders ev - er on its way, Does wan - der

wan - der free? Tra la la, Tra la la, Tra la la la
on its way. Tra la la, etc.

la la, Tra la la Tra la la, Tra la la la la.

3 We see it in the mill-wheels, too :
They ne'er repose, and ne'er delay,
They weary not the live-long day,
The mill-wheels all the day.   Tra la la, etc.

4 The stones, too, heavy though they be,
Round in the giddy circle dance,
E'en fain more quickly would advance,
The stones, too, would advance.   Tra la la, etc.

5 To wander, then, is my delight:
Oh, master, help me on my way,
Let me in peace depart today,
To wander, wander free.   Tra la la, etc.

LO! THE BLITHESOME LARK.

1. Lo! the blithesome lark is soar - ing Far a - loft in morning skies;
2. Ev - 'ry mountain al - tar blaz - es; In-cense sweet to heav'n as-cends;

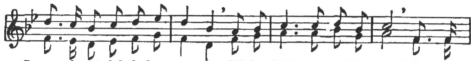

Songs of grateful gladness pouring, Higher, high - er, see him rise! Thousand
Meadows waft their silent praises; Ev-'ry flow'r a-dor-ing bends. Man, a-

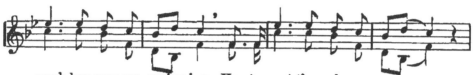

warb-lers now are spring-ing, Up to meet the welcome morn;
wake from heav-y slum - bers; Morning breaks serene - ly bright;

Sky and grove with joy are ring - ing; Hark the wild, en-tranc-ing horn.
Songs of praise, in tune-ful num-bers, Raise to Him who rules the night.

THE SHOWER.

RATHER SLOW.

1. See! the rain is fall - ing On the mountain's side;
2. See! the cool - ing show - er Comes at God's com-mand,

See the clouds be - stow - ing Bless - ings far and wide!
Bright-ens ev - 'ry flow - er, Cools the heat - ed land.

KEY OF E-FLAT.

The pupils will observe that the new chromatic sound used in the formation of this key is a-flat (or, in singing, aes).

This diagram appears upon the staff, thus:

The following exercise in three-four time, including the dotted quarter-note followed by an eighth note, as in the second measure, is repeated here, because it is one of the most difficult forms of measure to be met with, that appears so easy. The universal tendency is to sing the third note too soon.

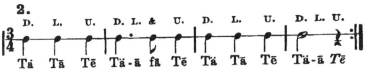

THE BELL.

1. Bell, thy tone is cheer-ful, When the bri - dal par - ty
2. Bell, thy tone is peace-ful, When it bids us gath - er

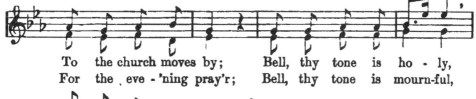

To the church moves by; Bell, thy tone is ho - ly,
For the eve - 'ning pray'r; Bell, thy tone is mourn-ful,

When on Sab - bath morn - ing Fields de - sert - ed lie.
Toll - ing for the lov'd ones Who de - part - ed are.

3 Say, how canst thou mourn so?
  How canst thou rejoice, too,
    Lifeless as thou art?
  All our joys and sorrows
  Graciously thou sharest,
    Speaking to the heart!

4 God has wondrous power,
  That we understand not,
    Given thee, sweet bell!
  When the heart is failing,
  Thou dost give it comfort,
    Soothing like a spell.

SHARP-FOUR IN THE KEY OF E-FLAT.

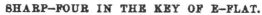

5   8   7   6   5   #4   5   5   3   4   5   6   7   8
bes   es   d   c   bes   a   bes   bes   g   aes   bes   c   d   es

GERMAN CHORAL IN THE KEY OF E-FLAT.

SHARP—FOUR IN THE KEY OF E.

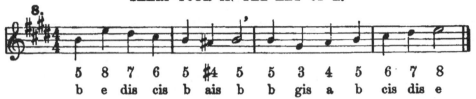

5	8	7	6	5	♯4	5	5	3	4	5	6	7	8
b	e	dis	cis	b	ais	b	b	gis	a	b	cis	dis	e

THE PRECEDING CHORAL IN THE KEY OF E.

THE FOUNTAIN.

1. Bubbling Spring, so bright and clear, Pleas-ant is thy voice to hear;
2. Oft at noon-day's sul-try heat, We have sought thy cool re-treat;

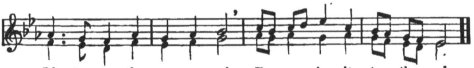

Lis - ten to the song we raise, For we sing it to thy praise.
And be - side the sha - dy pool Sipp'd the wa - ter clear and cool.

3 On thy margin's grassy mound
Are the earliest violets found;
And our wreath-crown'd heads we view,
Pictured in thy mirror true.

4 Thou dost never idly stay
Ling'ring on thy chosen way;
All, like thee, are onward driven,
Nought is firmly fix'd but heaven.

10.

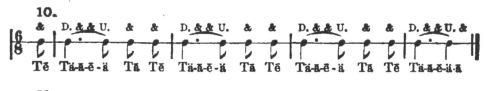

Tĕ Tä-ä-ĕ-ä Tă Tĕ Tä-ä-ĕ-ä Tă Tĕ Tä-ä-ĕ-ä Tă Tĕ Tä-ä-ä-ä

11.

THE WILD BIRD'S SONG.

C. M. Von Weber.

GENTLY, SLOWLY.

1. I ride .. up - on .. the green tree - tops
2. I sing .. I sing . of my Mak - er's

high . . When parch'd is the earth and the brook - lets are
love, . . The wan - der-er stops near my shel - ter - ing

dry; I sing, . . I sing in my cov - ert
grove; He hears . . the song in the qui - et

cool And lave . . my breast in the calm shad-y pool.
air, And list - ens and smiles, and for - gets all his care.

3 At night to my sheltering pine I fly,
    And sleep till the day-dawn gilds the sky;
    Then loud I sing from a swelling breast,
    In praise of the God who protects my nest.

THE GOOD NEIGHBOR.

Old German.

SLOWLY.

1. Dear neigh-bor, pray lend me your lan-tern to-night;
2. Yes, neigh-bor, I'll lend you my lan-tern to-night;

The sky is so dark, and the stars give no light;
It storms, it is dark, and the moon gives no light;

My shep-herd has lost my best lambs by the way,
And tho' it be brok-en, no fault will I find,

And I must go with him and find where they stray.
For fast it is rain-ing, and cold is the wind!

3 Good neighbor, should trouble your path e'er betide,
Then pray call upon me, and be not afraid;
The few transient sorrows that press us to-day,
By helping each other, will soon pass away.

WILD-WOOD FLOWERS.

Dr. LOWELL MASON.

1. Flow-ers, wild-wood flow-ers, In a shel-ter'd dell they grew;

Flow-ers, wild-wood flow-ers, In a shel-ter'd dell they grew;

I hur - ried a - long, and I chanc'd to spy This small star-

flow'r with its sil - v'ry eye; Then this blue dai - sy peep'd up its

head, Sweet - ly this pur - ple or - chis spread. We

gath-er'd them all for you, We gath-er'd them all for

you; All these wild - wood flow - ers, Sweet wild - wood

flowr's, All these wild-wood flow - ers, Sweet wild-wood flow'rs.

2 |: Flowers, lovely flowers,
    In the garden we may see. :|
The rose is there with her ruby lip,
    With pinks,—the honey we love to sip,
Tulips, gay as a butterfly's wing,
Marigolds rich as the crown of a king,
|: But none so fair to me .|
As these wild-wood flowers, etc.

KEY OF A-FLAT.

[The entire class will carefully sing the following exercise.]

8. PREPARATORY TO " ARRIVAL OF SPRING."

SLOWLY.

ARRIVAL OF SPRING.

LIVELY.

1. The Spring, the mer - ry Spring is come; Who would her beauties see,
2. Con-cealed a - mid the   for - est deep All Win - ter hath she lain;

Oh, let him quick-ly   forth to roam, The mead-ow-flow'rs to   see!
A bird hath roused her from her sleep, And now she's here a - gain.

8 The Spring returns again to cheer
 With joy and merry song;
 Where'er her beauteous charms appear,
 Delights around her throng.

4 Then forth into the meadows green,
 And let us freely roam;
 When first the coming Spring is seen,
 Oh, who would stay at home?

————————

9.

SWEET SPRING.

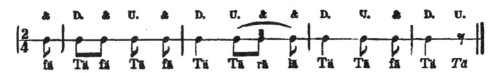

F Ziska.

1. Sweet Spring is re - turn - ing; She breathes on the plain,
2. Full glad - ly I greet thee, Thou lov - li - est guest!

And mead - ows are bloom - ing In beau - ty a - gain.
Ah, long have we wait - ed By thee to be blest;

Now fair is the flow - er And green is the grove,
Stern Win - ter threw o'er us His heav - y, cold chain;

And soft is the show - er That falls from a - bove.
We love to be breath - ing In free - dom a - gain.

3 And then, O thou kind one,
  Thou camest so mild,
And mountain and meadow
  And rivulet smiled;
The voice of thy music
  Was heard in the grove;
The balm of thy breezes
  Invited to rove.

4 Now welcome, thou loved one,
  Again and again,
And bring us full many
  Bright days in thy train;
And bid the soft Summer
  Not linger so long,
And bid the soft Summer
  Not linger so long.

ARISE, ARISE.

Dr. J. MAINZER.

1. Rise, rise, my boy! yon splen-did ray, Fore - tells a long and
2. Rise, rise, my boy! the wood-man's gone, To range the wood-land
3. Rise, rise, my boy! the bus - y bee Flies round and round the
4. Rise, rise, my boy! nor lon - ger keep Thy sen - ses locked in

love - ly day; The world's a - wake, and all the wise Im -
wilds a - long; And o'er the hill and mountain's height He
li - lac tree; The lark and thrush, all birds, a-wake And
sloth-ful sleep, O yield not thus to slum - ber's pow'r Nor

prove this hour; a - rise, a - rise; The world's awake, and all the wise Im-
trudg - es on with heart so light; And o'er the hill and mountain's height He
flut - ter o'er the mountain-lake; The lark and thrush, all birds, awake And
waste the day's most precious hour, O yield not thus to slumber's pow'r, Nor

prove this hour; a - rise, a - rise, a - rise, a - rise, a - rise, a -
trudg-es on with heart so light, with heart so light, with heart, with
flut-ter o'er the mountain lake, the moun-tain lake, the lake, the
waste the day's most pre-cious hour, most pre - cious hour, the day's most

rise, a - rise, a - rise, a - rise, a - rise.
heart so light, with heart, with heart so light.
moun - tain lake, the lake, the moun - tain lake.
pre - cious hour, the day's most pre - cious hour.

SWISS HERDSMAN'S SONG.

From the French.+

ADAGIO.

1. Now breaks the morn: Ye herds - men, wak - en!

Sweet - ly the horn, Re-sounds a - far. Ho - la, Ho - la,

herds - men, wak - en! Morn - ing has come. . .

Herds - men, wak - en, Morn-ing has come! See the herds

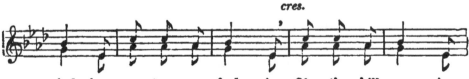

wind - ing, pas - tur - age find - ing; O'er the hills go - ing,

List to their low - ing. White, black, and red ones, Sleek and well

fed   ones, Spot - ted and stri - ped, Come, by our   cry   led.

ADAGIO.

Herds - men, wak   en, Morn - ing has   come! . .

Herds - men, wak - en, Morn - ing has come.

VIVACE.

Bells, tink - ling gai · ly, Glad - den us   dai - ly;

Peace · ful our days go, 'Neath the sun's rays. Oh!

ADAGIO.

Herds - men, wak - en, Morn - ing has   come!

Herds - men,   wak - en, Morn - ing has come!

On page 76, attention has been called to the fact that, starting from the key of C, every time a new sharp was added to form the scales in the keys of G, D, A, and E, the new key was based on the fifth of the scale preceding it, and that the keys in which flats were used were based on the fourth of the scale preceding. The following exercises are in illustration of the above.

GOING FROM ONE KEY TO ANOTHER.—BY SHARPS.

PART III.—MISCELLANEOUS PIECES.

GRANDMOTHER'S ADVICE.

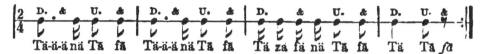

Tä-ä-änä Ta fä   Tä-ä-änä Ta fä   Tä za fä nä Ta fä   Tä   Ta *fa*

From the French. +
SLOWLY AND QUIETLY.

1. Maid - ens, if you'd have me praise you, Do your work with nim-ble
2. Dal - ly not, nor waste the mo-ments, Steps grow man-y, feet grow

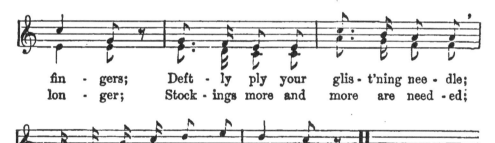

fin   - gers;   Deft - ly   ply   your   glis - t'ning nee - dle;
lon   - ger;   Stock - ings more and   more   are   need - ed;

Time for   i - dlers nev - er   lin - gers.
Nim-bly   knit them strong and strong - er.

3 Seek a method in your life-work,
  Ev'ry fit occasion seizing ;
Count each word and step, like knitting,
  Then shall speech and work be pleasing.

4 Mend the rents while they are little,
  Ere they grow beyond your power:
Cure your faults of tongue and temper,
  Ere they pass youth's tender hour.

LOVE OF TRUTH.

1. My days of youth, tho' not from fol - ly free,   I
2. My foot - steps lead,   O Truth, and mould my will,   In

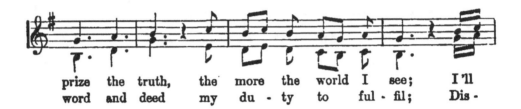

prize the truth,   the more the world I   see;   I 'll
word and deed   my du - ty to   ful - fil;   Dis -

keep the straight and nar - row path, And, lead wher - e'er   it
hon - est acts, and sel - fish aims To truth can ne'er be -

may, The voice of   truth I 'll fol - low and o - bey.
long; No deed of mine, shall be   a   deed of wrong.

3 The strength of youth, we soon see it decay,
   But strong is truth, and stronger ev'ry day,
      Though falsehood seem a mighty pow'r
         Which we in vain assail,
   The power of truth will in the end prevail.

4 My days of youth, tho' not from folly free,
   I prize the truth, the more the world I see;
      I 'll keep the straight and narrow path,
         And, lead where'er it may,
   The voice of truth I 'll follow and obey.

COLD THE BLAST MAY BLOW.

German.

1. Cold the blast may blow,　Heap - ing high the
1. Cold the blast may blow,

2. Bo - soms firm and bold　Fear not wind nor
2. Bo - soms firm and bold

snow;　Winds may loud - ly roar, ... may
Heap - ing high the　snow,　Winds may loud - ly roar;
cold,　Fear not ice nor snow, ... not
Fear not wind nor　cold,　Fear not ice nor snow;

loud - ly roar;　Trees, all brown and bare,　Sad may wave in
ice nor snow;　Fierce-ly thro' the gale　Drift the snow and

air,　Deck'd with leaves no more,　Deck'd with leaves no more.
hail;　Hearts may warm - ly glow,　Hearts may warm-ly glow.

3 When in school we meet,
　Looks of welcome greet,
　　Sent |: from smiling eyes ; :|
　When our teachers dear
　Give us words of cheer,
　　|: What are wintry skies! :|

4 Come, then, rain or hail,—
　Come, then, storm or gale,—
　　Glad |: to school we 'll go ; :|
　Bosoms firm and bold
　Shrink not from the cold,—
　　|: Fear not ice nor snow. :|

MORNING DEVOTION.

NAGELL

1. How sweet from gloom-y dark - ness The blush - ing morn a-
2. While in the ear - ly sun - shine The sil - ver dew - drops

wakes! How rich the ear - ly mu - sic That
gleam, And ev - 'ry thing re - joic - es In

from the for - est breaks! Sure na - ture, all so
morn - ing's gold - en beam; With warm de - vo - tion

love - ly, Its Mak - er's good - ness feels, Which floats in
glow - ing, A - wake, my soul, and pay To God thy

all the breez - es, And ev - 'ry bless - ing seals.
grate - ful wor - ship, Who made the love - ly day.

3 My Father, give me power
To consecrate to thee
My life, and every blessing
That is conferred on me;
Let wisdom guide my conduct,
Let all my days be peace;
And when my life is ended,
Receive my soul to bliss.

WHEN THE DAY WITH ROSY LIGHT.

1. When the day with ro - sy light, In the morn-ing glad ap-pears,
2. Oh! 'tis sweet at ear - ly day Then to climb the moun-tain-side,

And the dusk-y shades of night Melt a - way in dew-y tears,
Where the mer-ry song-ster's lay Sweet-ly ech oes - far and wide:

Up the sun-ny hills I roam, Bid good-mor-row to the flow'rs,
Noon may have its sun-ny glare; Eve, its twi-light and its dew;

Wak - en, in their high-land home, The minstrels of the bow'rs.
Night, its soft and cool-ing air;—But give me morn - ing blue.

Tra la la la la la la la, Tra la la la la la la la,

Tra la la la la la la la Tra la la la la la.

THE FARMER'S BOY.

1. The Sun had sunk be - hind the hills A - cross yon drear - y moor,
2. My fa-ther's dead,my moth - er's left With four poor child-ren small,

When wet and cold there came a boy, Up to the far-mer's door:
And what is worse for moth-er still, I'm el - dest of them all.

Can you tell me, said he, If an - y there be Who would
But, tho'young, I will work As hard as I can, If I

like to give em - ploy, For to plough and to sow, For to
once can get em - ploy, For to plough, etc.

reap and to mow, For to be a far - mer's boy, . .

For to be a far - mer's boy.

3 But if no boy you chance to want,   And at break of the day I'll trudge
   One favor I would ask,—   far away,
To shelter me till dawn of day,   And will elsewhere seek employ.
   From the cold and wintry blast,   For to plough, etc.

[Concluding stanzas on opposite page.]

IN THE COTTAGE WHERE WE DWELL.

MODERATO.

1. In the cottage where we dwell, We have led a   peace - ful life;
2. Blest with life and blest with health, We de - sire no   rich - er home;
3. All the sweets of wealth will pall: Hon - est hearts and   lib - er - ty,

Ours are joys which none can tell, Who en - gage in   anx - ious strife;
Nor to be the slaves of wealth, Do we ev - er wish to roam;
In our cot are with them all, Home is home where e'er it be.

(1-3). Tho' but low - ly   be our state Yet con - ten - ted with our   lot

We en - vy not the proud and great, Happy in   our   humble lot.

[Concluded from opposite page.]

4 The Farmer's wife cries, Try the lad,
  Let him no further seek,
Oh, do, papa! the daughter cries,
  While tears run down her cheek;
For those that will work,'tis hard they
  should want,
Or should wander for employ.
  For to plough and to sow,
  For to reap and to mow,
    For to be, etc.

5 The farmer's boy, he grew a man;
  The good old farmer died:
He left the lad with all he had,
  And his daughter for his bride.
The boy that was, now a farmer is,
  And he thinks, and smiles with
    joy,
  On the break of the day,
  When he passed that way.
    For to be, etc.

HAPPINESS.

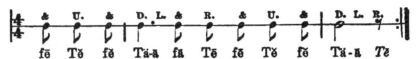

fē Tŏ fĕ Tä-ă fä Tŏ fĕ Tŏ fĕ Tä-ă Tĕ

Dr. J. Mainzer

1. True hap - pi - ness   is not the growth of earth,   The tri - al's
2. Sweet flowers of Par   -   a - dise! thy seeds are sown,   In here and

fruit - less if you seek it   here; 'Tis an ex - o - tic
there   a mind of heavenly   mold; It ris - es slow and

of ce - les - tial birth   And ne - ver blooms   but in   ce - les - tial
buds nev - er were known   To blos - som here,   the cli - mate is too

air,   And nev - er   blooms but in ce - les - tial   air.
cold,   To blos-som   here,   the cli - mate is   too   cold.

MY COUNTRY.

From the French. +

L. Kurz.

1. O my coun - try! fond - ly cher - ish'd, All my heart's af - fec - tion's

thine, Ar dent glow-ing, O - - ver-flow-ing

Ev - er-more with love di - vine,— Yes, ev - er-more.

2 O my country! all my life now
   Do I give thee, e'en to death;
   And the story
   Of thy glory
   Utter with my latest breath,—
   Yes, unto death.

3 O my country! be thou blesséd;
   Grant, O Lord, we dwell in peace;
   Save our nation,
   From temptation;
   To the bondsman give release,—
   Yes, glad release.

THE TWO VOICES.

From the French.+   B. WILHEM.
ANDANTE.

1. Sweet thro' the night Sound-eth the clear song Of the night-in-
2. Deep in my soul Sound-eth a sweet voice; I can hear it

Joy - ful and bright, . . . Borne by the
Glad ac-cents roll, ... Bid-ding my

gale in the wood;   Joy - ful and bright,   By
well, day and night;   Glad ac-cents bid   My

winds   a - long.
heart   re - joice.

winds borne a - long, It tell - eth of God, ev - er good.
sad heart re - joice: 'T is God fills my spir - it with light.

THE NATURAL.

(Teachers will excuse this repetition.

Besides the sharp (♯) and the flat (♭) which we have used, there is another character, called the natural, made thus : ♮. The natural is used to take away the effect of a sharp or flat ; for example :

| 5 | ♯4 | 5 | 4 | 3 | 2 | 1 | 5 | ♭7 | 6 | 7 | 8 | 7 | 8 |
| g | fis | g | f | e | d | c | g | bes | a | b | c | b | c |

SHARP—ONE.

| 7 | 8 | 2 | 2 | ♯1 | ♯1 | 2 | } Not difficult. |
| e | f | g | g | fis | fis | g | |

| 8 | 7 | 3 | } Difficult. |
| f | e | a | |

SOME DIFFICULT PLACES.

More difficult than it seems.
| 2 | 3 | 4 | 4 | 5 | 6 | 3 | 4 |
| g | a | bes | bes | c | d | a | bes |

THE HERDSMAN'S HAPPY HOME.

Poetry, Old English.   FRANZ SCHUBERT.

1. What pleas-ures have great prin - ces More dain-ty to their choice

Than herdsmen wild who care - less, In qui - et life re - joice,

In qui - et life re - joice?

2 All day their flocks each tendeth,
    All night they take their rest,
  More quiet, than who sendeth,
  |: His ship into the East. :|

3 Oh! happy who thus liveth,
    Not caring much for gold,
  With clothing which sufficeth
  |: To keep him from the cold. :|

EARLY SPRING DAYS.

FRANZ ABT.

SLOWLY.

1. Each whis - per of the wil - low, Each mur - mur of the pine,
2. Now through the sparkling wa - ters The fish - es glide a - long,

Each rip - ple of the bil - low, In joy - ful con - cert join.
And thro' the woodland ech - oes The bluebird's cheer-ful song.

3 The happy birds, with singing,
    The grove and forest cheer,
  From hill to dale repeating,
    The welcome Spring is here.

4 Each living thing rejoices
    In Him who made the Spring,
  We 'll shout with swelling voices;
    And cheerful praises sing.

THE VIOLET.

From the French.✛   R. Hotz.

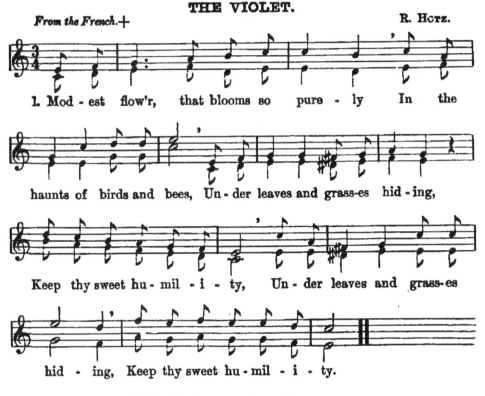

1. Mod - est flow'r, that blooms so pure - ly In the

haunts of birds and bees, Un - der leaves and grass-es hid - ing,

Keep thy sweet hu - mil - i - ty, Un - der leaves and grass-es

hid - ing, Keep thy sweet hu - mil - i - ty.

2 If the glowing sun alarms thee,
   In thy shy simplicity,
|: Thou art rendered still more charming
   By thy sweet humility. :|

3 Beaten by the storm, the lily
   Weeps at its severity;
|: And she longs, when bruised and broken,
   For thy sweet humility. :|

4 May I never wish for grandeur,
   Rather seek thy purity;
|: Ever have for my adorning,
   Only sweet humility. :|

5 O my Father, may my childhood
   Pass in sweet security,
|: In the modest ways of virtue,
   Guarded by humility. :|

THE RAMBLE.

J. A. FEBERER.

1. I've been sit-ting by the hill-side, Lit-tle birds flew gai-ly
2. I've been stand-ing in the gar-den, Where the buzz-ing bees flew

round; What a sing-ing, What a spring-ing From the
round: What a hum-ming, Go-ing, com-ing, As their

nest-lings to the ground! La, la, la, la, la, la, la,
hon-ey cells they found! La, la, la, la, la, la, la,

la, la, la, la, la, la, la. La, la, la, la,

la, la, la, la, la, la, la, la.

3 I've been walking in the meadow:
   Little swallows skimmed the brook;
What a dipping, what a dripping —
   Oh, how droll it made them look!
      La, la, la, etc.

4 Cheerful comrades soon will join us,
   With the sun's last parting ray;
Then with singing, voices ringing,
   We will close this happy day.
      La, la, la, etc.

SONG OF THE WOODS.

German Air.

1. Oh, could I in the greenwood be Thro' all the Sum-mer-time,
2. The branches beck-on me to stay Be-neath their sha-dy dome,

What pleas-ure would they give to me, Those trees in all their prime!
The mead-ow-flow-ers nod and say, "Come, gen-tle stran-ger come!"

8 The birds, awaken'd from their sleep,
    Are soaring high and free;
    The deer and roe with dancing step
    Are springing merrily.

4 Young birds from ev'ry twig and bough,
    Enchanted with their home,
    Are singing loud and singing low,
    "Come, seek the greenwood, come!"

NOW ALL AROUND IS BRIGHT.

SALTZBERG, 1810.

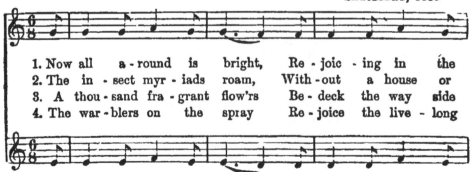

1. Now all a-round is bright, Re-joic-ing in the
2. The in-sect myr-iads roam, With-out a house or
3. A thou-sand fra-grant flow'rs Be-deck the way side
4. The war-blers on the spray Re-joice the live-long

light Of Sum-mer's gen - ial rays; A - bove no clouds are
home; They sport thro' their brief day; At morn they flut - ter
bow'rs Of nat - ure's ver - dant fields; The lim - pid lake and
day, On air - y seats a - bove; Oh, may we catch the

seen, Be - low all smiles se -
high, At ev'n - ing gen - tly
stream With hap - py creat - ures
strain, And ech - o it a -

1. A - bove no clouds are seen, Be - low all smiles se -
2. At morn they flut - ter high, At ev'n - ing gen - tly
3. The lim - pid lake and stream With hap - py creat - ures
4. Oh, may we catch the strain, And ech - o it a -

rene, Like child-hood's sun - ny days.
die: Like dew they pass a - way.
teem, And earth its in - cense yields.
gain, In har - mo - ny a - bove!

rene, Like child - hood's sun - ny . . days.
die: Like dew they pass a - way.
teem, And earth its in - cense yields.
gain, In har - mo - ny a - bove!

COMING OF SPRING.

German.

1. Your win-dows up! your hearts a-rouse! Come quick-ly! come
2. Your win-dows up! your hearts a-rouse! Come quick-ly! come

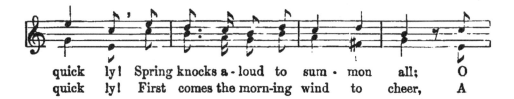

quick ly! Spring knocks a-loud to sum-mon all;   O
quick ly! First comes the morn-ing wind to cheer,   A

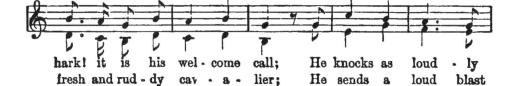

hark! it is his wel-come call;   He knocks as loud-ly
fresh and rud-dy cav-a-lier;   He sends a loud blast

as he may, With ti ny flow'r-buds in ar-ray.
thro' the air, His mas ter's com-ing to pre-pare.

3 Your windows up! your hearts arouse!
    Come quickly! come quickly!
Now comes the sunshine, gallant knight,
    With golden spear all glistening bright;
The breath of perfumed flowers sweet
    Steals through each narrow, still retreat.

4 Your windows up! your hearts arouse!
    Come quickly! come quickly!
Now calls the nightingale's glad song,
    And hark! oh, hark! an echo long
Within my breast is answering:
    Oh, welcome, welcome, joys of Spring!

THE CHASE.

1. The dusk-y night rides down the sky, And ush-ers in the morn;

The hounds all join in glo-rious cry, The hunts-man winds his horn.

When a-hunt-ing we do go, When a-hunt-ing we do go,

When a-hunt-ing, hunt-ing, hunt-ing we do go, . .

When a-hunt-ing, hunt-ing, hunt-ing we do go.

2 Sly Reynard he like lightning flies,
His cunning wide awake ;
To gain the race he eager tries,
His forfeit life the stake.
Cho.—When a-hunting, etc.

3 But now, his strength to faintness worn,
The hounds have seized their prey;
Then, hungry, homeward we return,
To hunt another day.
Cho.— When a-hunting, etc.

TRIPLETS IN THREE-FOUR TIME.

CEASE SWEET CONTENT TO SLANDER.

From " Guy Mannering."   FR. SCHUBERT.*

1. Cease sweet Con - tent to slan - der! More con - stant than the
2. But seek her in the cot tage Of some se - clud - ed

dove, She ne'er was given to wan-der From home-born peace and love; Oh,
dell; 'T is neath its peace-ful shel-ter She most is wont to dwell; She

't is not in the pal - ace That joys like her's a -
loves to soft en sor - row, To drive each care a -

bound; 'T is not midst wealth and glo - ry And fame that she is
way, And o'er the hour of dark-ness, To shed a cheering

found, And fame that she is found.
ray, To shed a cheer - ing ray.

*FRANZ SCHUBERT, when a boy of eleven, lived in Vienna at the time Beethoven was in his prime. He began to write music, both vocal and instrumental, when very young. In all his compositions there are difficult places, more so than at first appears. In this song, the chief difficulty is in the time — particularly in the measures containing triplets, which will require special attention. The difficulties in both time and tune will be best overcome by first studying well the exercises 2 a and 2 b, on page 118, carefully beating the time and using the time-names.

SPRING SONG.

ANDRE.

ALLEGRETTO.

1. The heav-ens are smil-ing so soft and so blue, The hills and the

mead-ows all glit - ter with dew, The trees wave their blos-soms, so

fra-grant and fair, And sweet warbling songsters are fill-ing the air.

2 We 'll off to the woods and leave sorrow at home;
  We 'll climb the green hills, for 't is pleasure to roam.
  Oh! who in the city would stay the year round,
  When pleasures like these are so easily found?

3 But ah, the sweet flowers but bloom for a day!
  See! many have fallen and sprinkled our way:
  They fall in light showers, if branches but wave,
  And strew the lone violet's balmiest grave.

4 So all things must feel the cold finger of death!
  The strongest must fall, and must yield up their breath;
  The fate of the monarch is seen in the rose,
  And ours is the slenderest blossom that grows.

5 But death has no terrors to those who do right:
  To them he appears like an angel of light,
  And smilingly beckons their spirits away
  To realms of unending, unspeakable day.

THE ALPINE SHEPHERD.

GREITH.

1. From hills with snow-peaks heav'nward tending, Lit up by ro - sy
2. Here dwell I free and far from sor - row, And breathe the healthy

dawn, Lit up by ro - sy dawn, Ha - li ha - li
air; And breathe the health - y air; Ha - li ha - li

ha - li ha - li ho! My song of praise is now as-
ha - li ha - li ho! I am not anx - ious for the

cend-ing, To greet the com - ing morn, To greet the com - ing
mor-row, Nor know a thought of care, Nor know a thought of

morn. Ha - li ha - li ha - li ho, ha - li ha - li .. ho!
care. Ha - li ha - li ha - li ho, ha - li ha - li .. ho!

8 At eve, beneath the starry heaven,
‖: I seek my humble cot, :‖ Hali hali, etc.
And praise His name, who thus has given
‖: The joy that crowns my lot. :‖ Hali hali, etc.

TO THE LARK.

DR. J. MAINZER.

1. Pret-ty lark, thy cheer-ful lay Wel-comes in the dawn-ing

day; Nat-ure's morn-ing hymn is heard First from

thee, de - light - ful bird, First from thee, de - light - ful bird.

2 Thou art mounting to the sky
   While thy notes are heard on high,
   And, so rapid is thy flight,
 |: Thou wilt soon be out of sight. :|

3 As thou mountest to the skies,
   May I in true virtue rise,
   Seeking Wisdom's perfect ways,
 |: To direct my future days. :|

HARVEST'S REWARD.

From the French. +   L. KURZ.

1. Al - read - y fields and plains are glow - ing, Bright in the sun;

The wind is o'er the cornfield blow - ing, Hay-time is be - gun.

2 The farmer, joyful with his neighbor,
   Sees that his field
   Will in return for honest labor
   Golden fruitage yield.

3 So he whose earnest hands, unceasing,
   Work with a will,
   Shall see his sure reward increasing,
   And life's garners fill.

WANDERING SONG.

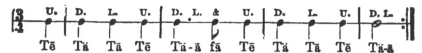

1. The sky is so clear, and all na - ture so
2. With pack on my back, and with staff in my

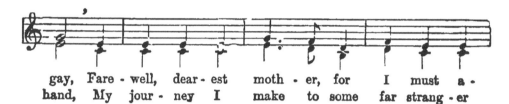

gay, Fare - well, dear - est moth - er, for I must a -
hand, My jour - ney I make to some far strang - er

way! Fare - well, dear - est moth - er, for I must a - way!
land: My jour - ney I make to some far strang - er land.

8 Beyond the wide plains, on the banks of the Rhine,
｜: Shall fortune and riches be speedily mine. :｜

4 One night you 'll be sitting all weary and lone,
｜: And thinking in tears of the wandering one; :｜

5 A tap at the window, a knock at the door —
｜: Your son is returned, to depart nevermore. :｜

6 "God bless thee, dear mother!" delighted, he cries,
｜: And empties his treasure before her glad eyes; :｜

7 "See, see! I have earned, by the work of my hand,
｜: This gold, dearest mother, for thee to command!":｜

SONG OF PRAISE.

(May be transposed to the key of B-flat.)

H. G. NÆGELI.

1. Oh, praise the Lord! He loves to hear you sing - ing;
2. We're heard a - far In God's most ho - ly dwell - ing,

In sweet ac - cord, Loud let his praise be ring - ing;
So loud and clear Our voic - es now are swell - ing;

Oh, praise the Lord! Oh, praise the Lord!
We're heard a - far, We're heard a - far.

3 Our voices raise,
　　With joy and gladness singing,
And cheerful praise,
　　Oh, let us all be bringing!
　　‖: Our voices raise! :‖

4 We bless thee, Lord,
　　While ev'ry heart rejoices ;
Thy name adored
　　We sing with falt'ring voices;
　　‖: We bless thee, Lord! :‖

5 Then evermore,
　　In ev'ry land and nation,
Tell o'er and o'er
　　The story of salvation.
　　‖: For evermore. :‖

THE SHEPHERD-BOY.
(May be transposed to the key of B-flat or A.)

F. ZISKA.

1. A moun-tain shep-herd-boy am I, I live a-
2. And here the stream-let mur-murs first, Whose wa-ters

bove the world so high; Here first the sun his
quell my burn-ing thirst; It pours o'er crag. thro'

beams dis-plays; Here lin-ger last his set-ting
rock-y nook;— I love, I love the moun-tain

rays; My home is on the moun-tain!
brook! My home is on the moun-tain!

3 The mountain is the home I love,
　Where angry tempests rage above;
　When their loud blasts the world appall,
　My soul shall rise above them all.
　　　　　My home is on the mountain!

4 And when fierce thunders roll around,
　I stand above the crashing sound—
　I call aloud and bid them cease:
　"Oh, leave my house in tranquil peace,—
　　　　　My home is on the mountain!"

5 And when the storm-clouds first appear,
　And lightning flashes through the air,
　I wander to the vale below,
　So gaily singing as I go.
　　　　　My home is on the mountain!

THE WORM.

COMMENCING WITH, fĕ, Tŏ fĕ; OR, AFTER THE RIGHT-BEAT IN
FOUR-FOUR TIME.

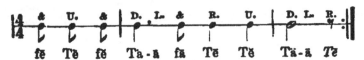

fĕ   Tŏ   fĕ   Ta-a   fă   Tĕ   Tŏ   Tä-ä   Tĕ

1. Turn, turn thy has   ty foot a   side,   Nor   crush that help-less
2. Let it en - joy   its lit - tle day,   Its   hum - ble bliss re -

worm: The frame thy thoughtless looks   de   ride,   Re - quired a
ceive,   Oh!   do not light - ly take   a   way,   The life thou

God   to   form,   Re quired   a   God   to   form.
canst   not   give,   The   life   thou   canst   not   give.

THE BEE'S LESSON.

(May be transposed to key of B-flat.)

MODERATELY FAST.

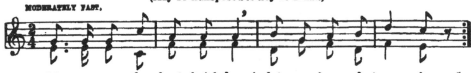

1. { Lis - ten to   the bee's brisk hum! let us hear what says she:— }
   { "Lit tle folks, I   won - der much that you are so   la - zy; }

Work and ac - tion make our lives bright and hope-ful   ev - er;

When one ef - fort fails,—why, then make a new en - deav - or.

2 "Little folks, I wonder much that you will be wrangling;
Joy and peace will flee away, where there's alway jangling,
Our contented little home has no brawler in it,—
If there were one, he would be banished in a minute.

3 "Little folks, I wonder much that you 're so unruly,
Caring not for Him who has cared for you so truly.
We obey our lady-queen and with love attend her,
And from harm and injury with our lives defend her."

FALSE PRIDE.

TREVES, 1812.

1. How proud we are, how fond to show   Our clothes, and call them rich and

new,   When   the   poor sheep and silk - worm wore   That

ver - y cloth-ing long be - fore, That ver y cloth-ing long be - fore.

2 The tulip and the butterfly
Appear in gayer clothes than I;
Let me be dress'd fine as I will,
:Flies, worms, and flow'rs exceed me still. :

3 Then will I set my heart to find
Inward adornings of the mind
Love, knowledge, virtue, truth, and grace,—
:These are the robes of richest dress. :

THE BUGLE'S SONG.

CARL KELLER.

1. How sweet-ly swell, Thro' wood and dell, The bu-gle's sil - ver
2. Each list-'ning ear Is still, to hear The note so clear - ly

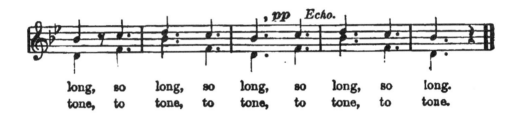

song! The ech - oes round Send back the sound, And speak so long, so
blown; While rocks a-round Send back the sound, And an-swer tone to

long, so long, so long, so long, so long.
tone, to tone, to tone, to tone, to tone.

3 Each leaf is still,
   Through dale and hill;
The birds to carol cease;
   The bubbling stream
   Would, list'ning, seem
To flow in peace, in peace, etc.

4 O'er hills and plains
   A Sabbath reigns;
Then own its soothing pow'r;
   All self forego,
   And, bowing low,
Be silent and adore, adore, etc.

THE NIGHTINGALE'S ANSWER.

German Air

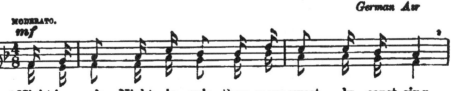

1. Night-in - gale, Night - in - gale, thou more sweet - ly canst sing,
   Night-in - gale, Night - in - gale, all do list to thy lay,

sweet - ly canst sing, Than ev - 'ry oth - er bird;
list to thy lay, When - ev - er thou dost sing.

When thou sing - est, all the world doth cry, Now comes

Spring so long de - ferred! Night-in gale, Night-in - gale, all do

list to thy lay, list to thy lay, Wher ev - er it is heard.

2 Nightingale, Nightingale, why so |: silent art thou? :|
    Why sing so short a song?
Nightingale, Nightingale, wherefore |: sing'st thou no more? :‖
    We for thy music long.
     When thou singest, all are full of joy;
     All our hearts grow firm and strong;
Nightingale, Nightingale, wherefore |: sing'st thou no more? :‖
    We for thy music long.

3 When the May, when the May, when the |: bright, merry May, :‖
    With buds and flower's, is o'er.
Then my heart, then my heart all so |: sorrowful is, :‖
    That I can sing no more.
     Not a single song can give me joy,
     As they always did before;
Yes, my heart, yes, my heart all so |: sorrowful is, :‖
    That I can sing no more.

THE SPARROW.

Dr. J. MAINZER.

1. The spar-row builds her lit - tle nest Of wool and hay and
2. Who taught the bus - y bee to fly A- mong the sweet - est

moss; Who taught her how to weave it best, And
flow'rs, And lay her stores of hon - ey by, To

lay the twigs a - cross? Who taught her how to weave it
last thro' Win - ter's hours, And lay her stores of hon - ey

best, And lay the twigs a - cross? Who taught her how to
by, To last thro' Win - ter's hours, And lay her stores of

weave it best, And lay the twigs a - cross?
hon - ey by, To last thro' Win - ter's hours.

3

Who taught the little ant the way
  Its winter home to bore,
And through the pleasant summer day
  To gather up its store,
|:And thro' the pleasant summer day,
  To gather up its store?:|

4

'Twas God who taught them all the way,
  And gave to them their skill,—
Who teaches children when they pray,
  To do his holy will;
|:Who teaches children, when they pray,
  To do his holy will.:|

THE BLIND BOY.

OLD GERMAN.

MODERATO.

1. It is not that I can-not see The birds and flow'rs of
2. They tell me that the birds whose notes Fall full up-on my

Spring; 'Tis not that beau-ty seems to me A
ear Are not all beau-ti-ful to sight, Tho'

dream - y, un - known thing; It is not that I
sweet their songs to hear, They tell me that the

can - not mark the blue and star - ry sky, Nor
gay - est flow'rs, Which sun - shine ev - er brings, Are

o - cean foam, nor mountain peak, That e'er I weep and sigh.
not the ones .I know so well, But strange and scent-less things.

4 My little brother leads me forth,
  To where the violets grow;
His gentle, light, and careful step,
  And tiny hand, I know;
My mother's voice is sweet and low,
  Like music on my ear;
The very atmosphere seems love,
  When they to me are near.

4 My father twines his arms around,
  And draws me to his breast,
To kiss his poor, blind, helpless boy;
  He says he loves me best.
'Tis then I ponder unknown things,
  It may be, weep or sigh,
And think how glorious it must be,
  To meet affection's eye!

THE RAIN.

(May be transposed to F.]

SCHADE.

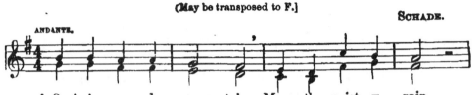

1. See! o'er yon - der moun - tains Moves the mist - y rain,
2 Rich or poor, what mat - ter? Each is here for good:

Pass - ing, from heav'n's foun tains, Bless-ings on the plain.
Good seeds let him scat - ter In con - tent-ed mood.

Now's the time for grow - ing; Quick-ly, then, be sow - ing!
For ye share to - geth - er Sun-shine and wet weath - er:

Let the well-till'd field . . . Rich a - bun-dance yield.
Heav'n these bless-ings gives . . . To each one that lives.

3 Let the sage, so knowing,
  On his wisdom build ;
We, still planting, ploughing,
  Wait what God hath willed.

'T is while Heav'n befriendeth,
Rain and sunshine sendeth,
That the verdure thrives :
God the blessing gives.

THE GROVE.

C. M. Von Weber.

1. The grove, the grove, the grove, the grove, The
2. The world, the world, the world, the world, The

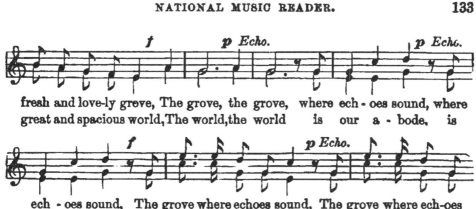

fresh and love-ly grove, The grove, the grove, where ech - oes sound, where
great and spacious world, The world, the world is our a - bode. is

ech - oes sound, The grove where echoes sound, The grove where ech-oes
our a - bode, The world is our a - bode, The world is our a -

sound, We hark to the note of the morn - ing horn, We
bode. We wan - der a - way thro' the fields so fair, We

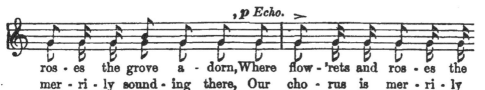

hark to the note of the morn - ing horn, Where flow - 'rets and
wan - der a - way thro' the fields so fair; Our cho - rus is

ros - es the grove a - dorn, Where flow - 'rets and ros - es the
mer - ri - ly sound - ing there, Our cho - rus is mer - ri - ly

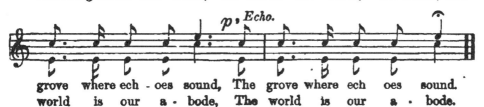

grove a - dorn. The grove, the grove, the grove, the grove, The
sound-ing there. The world, the world, the world, the world, The

grove where ech - oes sound, The grove where ech oes sound.
world is our a - bode, The world is our a - bode.

THE SWISS BOY.

GREITH.

1. { From pine-clad hills and moun-tains, My cher-ished childhood home,
   { A land of bless-ed free-dom, A gay Swiss boy, I come;

I glo-ry in my mountain-land, When on its snow-crown'd

heights I stand; From pine-clad hills and moun-tains, A

gay Swiss boy, I come. Tra la la la la la la

Repeat pp.

la la la, Tra la la la.

2 Among my merry comrades
  A joyous life I lead,
And in our verdant valleys
  No pain nor sorrow heed.
From hill and vale our songs we raise,
Our grateful songs of joy and praise;
From pine-clad hills and mountains,
  A gay Swiss boy, I come.
          Tra la la, etc.

SUMMER JOYS.

WM. B. BRADBURY.

1. Joy is warbling in the breez-es, Pleasures smile a - long the fields.

Na-ture, clad in robes of beau-ty, All . . . that's sweet and lovely yields.

Heav'n now sheds its mildest splen - dor O'er the land and o'er the deep;

In -sects feel the common pleas - ure,—Forth in hap-py crowds they creep

2 Humming bees and sailing swallows
  Gaily tell the lively glee
Nature's now so kindly shedding
  Over all the eye can see
" Welcome," says the flock that's feeding
  On the verdant, grassy hills;
" Welcome !" echoes many a songster,
  Chirping round the rippling rills.

3 Blooming flow'rs, their sweets exhaling,
  Join to make the charming scene
Yet still more like happy Eden,
  Ere the blight of human sin.
Glad we hail thee, lovely Summer,—
  Welcome, truly, is thy smile ;
Oh, that all like thee were lovely,
  Free from woe and free from guile !

CHANGES.

German Melody.
Fine.

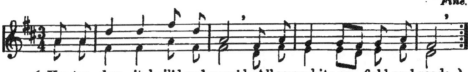

1. { Yes-ter-day it hail'd and snow'd; All was white on field and road; }
   { Now the snow is all a-way, And the hills are bare and gray. }

Oh, this life is ev-er chang-ing; All our pleasures melt a-way;

Hope a-lone re-mains, to prom-ise Some fut-ure, bright-er day.

2 Yesterday my great delight
   Was my rose-tree, fresh and bright;
   Now its faded flowers are shed;
   All may on my roses tread.
       Oh, this life, etc.

OH! THE LOVELY, LOVELY MAY.

German.

1. Oh, the love-ly month of May Ev-er wel-come, ev-er gay!
2. Oh, what verdure clothes the ground! Oh, what fragrance breathes around

When by vale and mountain,   When by brook and foun-tain,
See the wil-lows grow-ing   By the stream-let flow-ing,

Flow'rets bloom and in - sects play, In the love - ly, love - ly May.
See the grain is wav - ing high, 'Neath the blue and cloud-less sky

Oh, the love - ly, love - ly May, Ev - er wel - come, ev - er gay!

Charm-ing, charming, charming, charming, charm-ing, love - ly May!

3 Oh, how fresh the morning air!
Oh, how lovely all things are,—
Birds so gaily singing,
Woods and meadows ringing,
Buds and blossoms fresh and bright,
Leaves so green,—enchanting sight!
Oh, the lovely, etc.

4 Hark the universal shout!
Nature's fairest forms are out;
Lambs are playing, skipping,
Bees are buzzing, sipping;
Walk, or ride, or row the boat—
Stand, or fall, or sink, or float,—
Oh, the lovely, etc.

PICNIC SONG.

Join we now in mer-ry song, Voices ringing cheeri-ly,
While we roam the woods among, Gay and [*Omit* . . . .] free.

CONTENTMENT IS HAPPINESS,

German Air.

1. Yes, I am con - tent - ed, go things as they will,
2. Tho' no brill - iant torch - es on my sup - per shine,

Dwell - ing in my cot - tage, peace - ful - ly and still.
Tho' in cost - ly gob - lets spar - kle not the wine,

Ma - ny a fool has all things that his eyes be - hold,
I have what is need - ful, suf - fer not from dread;

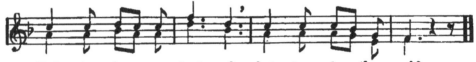

But to be con - tent - ed, bet - ter is than gold.
Noth - ing can taste sweet - er than my hard-earned bread.

3 Though my name be never heard in foreign land,
  Though no stars nor orders on my bosom stand,
  So my heart be noble, what were all the rest,—
  So my brother's welfare fill my humble breast?

4 I want no proud palace, want no stately hall;
  Brightly on my cottage heaven's sunbeams fall.
  Where content is dwelling, softly lies the head,
  Whether hard or downy be the sleeper's bed.

5 Though no costly marble will adorn my grave,
  Though above my coffin will no banners wave,
  Sacred peace will hover o'er my humble pall,
  And upon my green grave friendly tears will fall.

THE FOUNT OF JOY.

German.

CHEERFULLY.
Chorus.

1. { Joy, yes, joy 's the quick'ning stream, Which the whole earth wa - ters, }
   { Gladd'ning with its crys - tal gleam, All her sons and daugh-ters. }

Duet or Semi-Chorus.

What in val - ley blow - eth, What the hill - side show - eth,

Chorus.

Full of joy it glow - eth. There are stores of

joy to bless, And our dan - ger is ex - cess, And our

dan - ger is ex - cess, And our dan - ger is ex - cess.

2 Every one in his own way
   Eagerly pursues it:
But to seek is oft the way
   Certainly to lose it:
Happy he that knoweth
Where the true joy groweth,
And the false foregoeth.
   Yes, we 've stores of joy, etc.

WE KNOW A LAND.

H. G. NÆGELI.

1. We know a land of beau-ty's train, A-dorned with streams and
2. We know a land of vir-tue's growth, A land that no de-

groves and fields, Where clus-t'ring grapes and wav-ing grain The
cep-tion knows, A hap-py land, where love and truth Al-

ground in rich pro-fu - sion yields. This realm of beau-ty
lay the pain of earth - ly woes. This wor-thy land we

so well known Is but the land we call our own.
well may own; It is a land we call our own.

3 SOLO.—We know a land where moral light
      Has shed its hallowed influence round:
      Whose people know the God of might,
      And love the gospel's gladd'ning sound.
CHO.—This sacred land, so lovely shown,
      We surely may be proud to own.

4 SOLO.—We hail thee, Land so pure and great;
      With welcome honors thee we greet:
      Oh! may we ev'ry evil hate,
      That God may here maintain his seat.
CHO.—So shall we ever love to own
      That this great nation is our own.

MIDWINTER.

(May be transposed to Key of E-flat.)

F. GEYER.

COMMODO.

1. Now be - hold! now be - hold! See the snow, and feel how

LIGHTLY.

cold! Chil - dren, come, with joy and sing - ing, Where the

bright fire burneth, come! And while round your warm hearth springing, Think of

those who have no home, Thanking God! thanking God! thanking God!

2 Grateful be! grateful be for your mercies rich and free!
Oh, how many, poor and weary,
Sad and hungry, sick and cold,
Wander through this world so dreary,
Suff'ring more than can be told!
Grateful be! grateful be! grateful be!

3 Time improve! time improve! learn in youth to look above!
God will bless your pray'rful waiting,
And your pious deeds requite;
Doing good, and evil hating,
Are well pleasing in his sight.
Time improve! time improve! time improve!

COME, MAY, THOU LOVELY LINGERER.

ALLEGRETTO.   MOZART.

1. Come, May, thou love-ly lin-g'rer! And deck the groves a-gain,
2. True, win-ter days have man-y And man-y a dear de-light:

And let thy sil-v'ry stream-lets Me-an-der thro' the plain.
We fro-lic in the snow-drifts, And then—the Win-ter night,

We long once more to gath-er, The flow-'rets fresh and fair; . . .
A-round the fire we clus-ter, Nor heed the whistling storm; . .

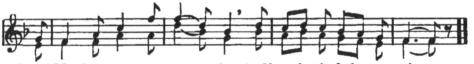

Sweet May! once more to wan-der, And breathe thy balm-y air.
When all with-out is drea-ry, Our hearts are bright and warm.

3 But oh, when comes the season
   For merry birds to sing,
How sweet to roam the meadows,
   And drink the breeze of Spring!

Then come, sweet May! and bring us
   The flow'ret fresh and fair;
We long once more to wander
   And breathe the balmy air.

PATRIOTIC SONG.

Scotch Air.

MAESTOSO.

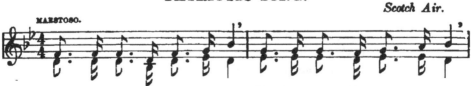

1. Friends, we bid you wel-come here. Freedom's sa-cred cause re-vere;
2. Who is he, de-void of shame, Jus-tice for him-self would claim,

Dai - ly breathe a pray'r sin-cere For them who suf - fer wrong.
Yet de - ny to all the same, Thro' vain and self - ish pride?

Fear not, lest your hope should fail, Truth is strong and must pre-vail;
Friends, you long our hearts have known; You're not left to fight a-lone;

What tho' foes our cause as - sail? They'll nev - er pros - per long.
We will make the cause our own, For Heav'n is on our side.

3 Who would live, to live in vain,   We would hope to leave behind
  Live alone for wordly gain,   Better times than now we find;
  Spending days and nights in pain   Better be it for mankind
    For some ignoble end ?   That we have lived their friend.

THE LARK POURS FORTH.

1- The lark pours forth a song of love, Her joy to tell, And

God, who hears it from a-bove, It pleas - eth well.

2 O'er ev'ry creature that doth fly,   3 Thy voice he hears, too, when outpour d
  Or walk, or creep,   In joy or woe,   [Lord
An ever-constant, watchful eye,   And though 't were mute, yet God the
  Their God doth keep.   Thy heart doth know.

COME, SEEK THE BOW'R.*

Dr. LOWELL MASON.

ALLEGRO.
1st Semi-Chorus.

1. Come, seek the bow'r, the ro - sy bow'r; I love its cool re -
2. Ye youths and maid - ens, join the song; I love a cheer - ful

2nd Semi-Chorus.

treat; The sun is high, and great his pow'r, And wea - ry
glee; The ech - oes shall our notes pro - long; Then come and

1st Semi-Chorus.

are our feet. Then Ed - ward and Em - ma, and
sing with me. Then Ed - ward and Em - ma, and

Jo-seph and Sar - ah, And Kit - ty, the beau - ti - ful maid,

2nd Semi-Chorus.

And Will - iam and Ma - ry, and Ro - bert and El - len, And

Full Chorus.

Rich-ard, the call o - beyed. Then Ed - ward and Em - ma, and

*The experimental introduction of music as a public-school study in Boston
occurred in December, 1837, under LOWELL MASON; and the result proved his

Jos-eph and Sar - ah, And Kit - ty, the beau - ti - ful maid,

And Will - iam and Ma - ry, and Rob - ert and El - len, And

Semi-Chorus.   The call o -

Rich-ard, the call o - bey'd, The call o - bey'd, . .

beyed.   The call o - beyed. *Full Chorus.*

. . The call o - bey'd, ... They

sought the bow'r, the ro - sy bow'r, And sat in the pleas - ant shade,

ad lib. a tempo.

They sought the bow'r, the ro - sy bow'r, And sat in the pleas-ant shade.

superior ability as a teacher in this field. The above piece was rendered in the first following exhibition of the Hawes School, South Boston, Aug. 14, 1838. Among the others were "Flowers, Wild-wood Flowers," page 92, and "Murmur, Gentle Lyre," page 147, of this book. The study was made general in 1839.

THE HARVEST TIME.

1. Thro' lanes with hedge-rows pearl - y   Go forth the reap - ers
2. At noon they leave the mead - ow,   Be - neath the friend - ly
3. And, when the west is burn - ing,   From shav - en fields re -

ear - ly,   A - mong the yel - low corn,   A-
sha - dow,   Of mon - arch oak to dine,   Of
turn - ing,   Up - on the train they come,   Up-

mong the yel - low corn. . .   Good luck be - tide their
mon - arch oak to dine, . .   And 'mid its branch - es
on the train they come; . .   And all their ham - let

shear - ing, For Win - ter now is near - ing, And
hoar - y Goes up a thank - ful sto - ry, The
neigh - bors, Re - joice to crown their la - bors, With

we must fill the barn, . . . And we must fill the barn.
har - vest is so fine, . . . The har - vest is so fine. . .
mer - ry har - vest home, . . With mer - ry har - vest home.

Tra la la la, Tra la la la, The bus - y har - vest time,
Tra la la la, Tra la la la, The bless - ed har - vest time,
Tra la la la, Tra la la la, The joy - ous har - vest time,

Tra la la la, Tra la la la, The bus - y har - vest time.
Tra la la la, Tra la la la, The bless - ed har - vest time.
Tra la la la, Tra la la la, The joy - ous har - vest time.

NIGHT SONG.

1. Mur - mur, gen - tle lyre, . . Thro' the lone - ly night;
2. Hark! the quiv - 'ring breez-es List thy sil - v'ry sound;

Let thy tremb-ling wire, . . Wa - ken dear de - light;
Ev - 'ry tu - mult ceas - es, Si - lence reigns pro - found;

Tho' the tones of sor - row, Min - gle with the strain,
Hush'd the thou-sand voic - es, Gone the noon-day glare;

Yet my heart can bor - row, Plea - sure from the pain.
Gen - tle spir - it - voic - es, Stir the mid - night air.

VACATION - SONG

1. A - way o - ver mountain, a - way o - ver plain; Va -
2. We've sought the ap prov - al of teach - ers and friends In

ca - tion has come with its pleasures a - gain; Where young steps are
climb-ing the path that to knowledge ascends; But now 'tis all

bound-ing, And young hearts are gay, To fun and to
o - ver, We'll off to our play, Nor think of our

frol - ic, a - way, boys, a - way! A - way! A -
books while from school we're a - way. To - day, To -

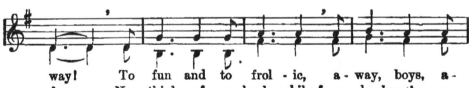

way! To fun and to frol - ic, a - way, boys, a -
day, Nor think of our books while from school we're a -

way! To fun and to frol - ic, a - way, boys, a - way!
way. Nor think of our books while from school we're a-way.

[Concluding stanzas on opposite page.]

CHEERFULNESS.

B. M. KOBLER

MODERATO.

1. It dear - ly ech - oes in the breast Like music's sweetest string; It
2. It gives us strength to do and bear; It makes the heavy light; It

warms our hearts with gen - tle glow, Like sun - ny days of Spring.
makes the rough - est pathway smooth, And cheers the darkest night.

8 It smiles within the clay-built hut,
  As in the princely dome:
  Sweet smiles of peace serene are seen,
  Where'er it makes its home.

4 This treasure rich is CHEERFULNESS,
  To willing bosoms given;
  From heavenly truth and good it flows,
  And turns again to heaven.

[Concluded from opposite page.]

3 The fresh breezes revel the branches between;
  The bird springs aloft from her covert of green;
  Our dog waits our whistle, the fleet steed our call;
  Our boat safely rocks where we moored her last fall,
      Our boat, our boat,
|: Our boat safely rocks where we moored her last fall. :|

4 Where clustering grapes hang in purple we know,—
  The pastures and woods where the ripe berries grow;
  The broad trees we'll climb where the sunny fruits rest,
  And bring down the stores for the lips we love best,
      Love best, love best,
|: And bring down the stores for the lips we love best. :|

5 Dear comrades, farewell! ye, who join us no more,
  Think life is a school, and, till term-time is o'er,
  Oh! meet unrepining each task that is given,
  And happy will end our probation in heav'n,
      In heav'n, in heav'n,
|: And happy will end our probation in heav'n. :|

THE BIRTH-DAY.

C. G. HERING.

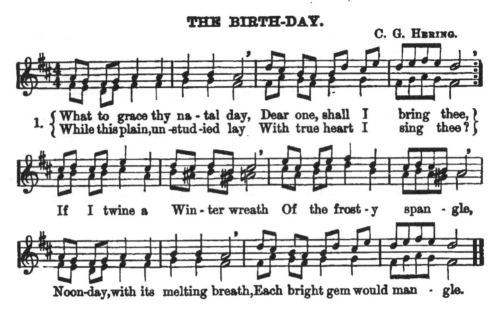

1. { What to grace thy na - tal day, Dear one, shall I bring thee, }
   { While this plain, un -stud -ied lay With true heart I sing thee? }

If I twine a Win - ter wreath Of the frost - y span - gle,

Noon-day, with its melting breath, Each bright gem would man - gle.

2 Buds that opened in the Spring
    Summer suns have faded;
Flow'rs that dropped from Summer's wing
    Autumn's fruit o'ershaded.
Summer stems, and Autumn fruit,
    Winter snows drift over;
Not a bud or leaf peeps out
    From the frosty cover.

3 Since, then, nature naught contains
    For a wreath to give thee,
Take what yet unchanged remains,—
    What can never leave thee:
Love that heeds not Winter's snow
    More than Autumn's shading—
Love which shall forever glow,
    Spite of frost and fading.

THE GROVE.

ANDANTE.

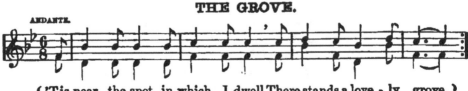

1. { 'Tis near the spot in which I dwell There stands a love - ly grove, }
   { En - compassed by a charming dell, In which I love to rove, }

To seek the gen - tle breez - es' sigh, And hear the feath-ered

song-sters' cry, Cuck - oo, cuck - oo, cuck - oo, cuck - oo, To

seek the gen - tle breez - es' sigh, And hear the feath - ered

song-sters' cry, Cuck - oo, cuck-oo, cuck - oo, cuck-oo, cuck - oo.

2 If days of sadness e'er assail,
    I hie me to the wood,
Where streams of pleasure never fail,
    Where all is bright and good:
'T is here, when no one else is nigh,
I hear the cuckoo's cheerful cry,
    Cuckoo, cuckoo, cuckoo, cuckoo,
        'T is here, etc.

3 When days of joy come o'er my head,
    I seek this charming scene,
Alone along the valley tread,
    And view the lively green;
And who so happy then as I,
In hearing oft the cheerful cry,
    Cuckoo, cuckoo, cuckoo, cuckoo,
        And who so happy, etc.

MERRILY EV'RY HEART IS BOUNDING.

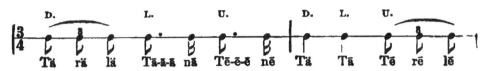

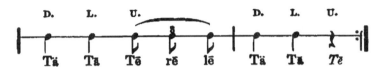

oh!   Mer - ri - ly   oh!   Mer - ri - ly, Mer - ri - ly, Mer - ri - ly

oh! . .   Mer - ri - ly   oh!   Mer - ri - ly   oh!

GOOD-NIGHT.

MODERATELY SLOW.

1. Good - night! good-night! Now to   all   a kind   good - night!
2. Good - night! good-night! Now to   all   a kind   good - night!
3. Good - night! good-night! Now to   all   a kind   good - night!

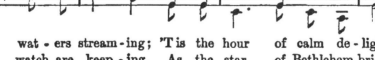

Lo!   the moon from heav'n is   beam - ing,   O'er   the   sil - ver
An - gel - like, while earth is   sleep - ing,   Stars   a - bove their
Slum - ber sweet - ly till the morn - ing,   Till   the sun, the

wat - ers stream - ing; 'T is the hour   of calm de - light. Good-
watch are keep - ing,   As the star   of Bethlehem bright. Good-
world a - dorn - ing, Rise in all   his glo-rious might! Good-

night! . .   Good - night! . .   Good - night!
night! . .   Good - night! . .   Good - night!
night! . .   Good - night! . .   Good - night!

BEFORE ALL LANDS IN EAST OR WEST.

1. Be - fore all lands in   east or west, I   love my na - tive
2. Be - fore all tongues in east or west, I   love my na - tive

land the best: With God's best gifts 't is teem - ing; For gold and
tongue the best: Tho' not so smooth-ly spok - en, Nor wov - en

jew - els here are found; And men of no - ble worth a-bound, And
with I - tal - ian art; Yet when it speaks from heart to heart, The

eyes of joy are beam - ing, And eyes of   joy are beam - ing.
word is nev - er brok - en, The word is   nev - er brok - en.

3 Before all people, east or west,
   I love my countrymen the best,
     A race of noble spirit:—
   A sober mind, a generous heart,
   To virtue trained, yet free from art,
   ‖: They from their sires inherit. :‖

4 To all the world I give my hand;
   My heart I give my native land,
     I seek her good, her glory;
   I honor ev'ry nation's name,
   Respect their fortune and their fame,—
   ‖: But *love* the land that bore me.:‖

PROCRASTINATION.

1. "Not to-day, we'll do it to-mor-row," La - zy peo - ple
2. But to-day's as good as to-mor-row; If you wait, 't will

say to their sor - row,"Yes, to - mor - row is the best;
be to your sor - row: Ev - 'ry day's its prop - er task.

Then, oh, then, how hard I'll la - bor!— But to - day my-
What is done, I see it plain - ly; What will come, I

self will fa - vor,—Yes, to - day I still will rest."
look for vain - ly, Then de - lay I'll nev - er ask.

3 This before us, that behind us,
  Each dull moment sharply reminds us
    Time that's lost is never found.
  What is floating down life's river,
  Take it, or its gone forever,—
    Moments lost are never found.

4 Ev'ry day I lose for to-morrow,
  In the book of life, to my sorrow
    Stands, a blank, unwritten page;
  Well, then, every day I'll labor,
  Help myself, and help my neighbor,
    In each work of love engage.

AT DISTRIBUTION OF PRIZES.

From the French. ✝
ALLEGRO MODERATO.

Immler.

1. Here rich and poor as-pire with e - qual right To win the
2. Yet rich - er rec-om-pense to him re - mains Who gives his

schol - ar's lau - rel crown, The fair a - ward of Jus - tice,
life to God a - bove; And no - bler yet the hope that

smil - ing bright, To Mer - it's prow - ess and re
in him reigns With sim - ple faith and hum - ble

nown, To Mer - it's prow - ess and re nown.
love, With sim - ple faith and hum - ble love.

3 To view th' eternal hill we sighing turn,
  While ev'ry grateful longing grows;
  So grace begets desires that stronger burn
  ‖: For ev'ry gift that God bestows. :‖

4 O glorious dwelling, city of our God,
  How beauteous are thy holy charms!
  Oh, may we gather in thy blest abode,
  ‖: And rest secure within thine arms. :‖

THE BEE IN FLOW'RY DELL.

SILCHER

MODERATO.

1. The bee, in flow-'ry dell, Is ev-er fly-ing
2. Who told the lit-tle bee That he could al-ways
3. 'T was God, the bees who taught; He hid the hon-ey

here and there, As if he nev-er tir-ed were, To
hon-ey find With-in each flow'r of ev-'ry kind, E-
in each flow'r, And there the bees may find their store, And

fill, to fill, to fill, to fill, to fill its lit-tle cell.
nough, e-nough, e-nough, e-nough, e-nough for him and me.
draw, and draw, and draw, and draw, and draw it free-ly out.

ON THE WATER.

VEAZIE.

BRISKLY.

Heave, yo ho!
Sail, sail, sail.

1. Up, up with the an-chor, boys, Yo-ho! heave, ho, yo-ho! The
2. Sail, sail now, my gal-lant bark, Sail on, sail on, sail on, We'll

sails are bent, and a-way we go, The white-caps gleaming brightly.
dash a-long with a mer-ry song, Each heart so gay and sprightly.

THE EVENING TWILIGHT.

German Air.

SOFT AND SLOW.

1. See! the sun is sink-ing fast, For the bus-y day is past;

Man from la-bor now doth haste, Peace-ful joys of home to taste.

2 Angels to watch o'er us now,
  Heav'nly Father, sendest thou!
  Guarded by their pow'r and might,
  We shall safely rest at night.

3 He whose eyes in sorrow weep,
  By sweet dreams is lulled to sleep;
  Angels kind, in visions bright,
  Lead him to the realms of light.

4 When our weary eyes shall close
  In the peaceful grave's repose,
  Then, O God, our guardian be,—
  Take our souls to dwell with thee.

5 When th' eternal morn shall break,
  And the dead from sleep awake,
  Take us to the realms above,
  To the home of joy and love!

RURAL DELIGHTS.

From "The Seasons."

Chorus.

1. Bright-ly, bright-ly gleam the spark-ling rills;

Sum-mer, Sum-mer sleeps on ver-dant hills;

Semi-Chorus.

A - mid the shades we, ramb-ling, stray, When cool - ing fountains

sport - ive play. Peal - ing, peal - ing, come the laugh and shout;

Chorus.

While gay - ly we sing, till the old for - ests ring, While

gay - ly we sing, till the old for - ests ring With the

joy of our mer-ry rout, With the joy of our mer - ry rout.

2 Odors, odors load the summer air,
   Music, music sweetly echoes there;
   And brightest maids, with softest glance,
   There join the song and lead the dance;
   Pealing, pealing come the laugh and shout,
      While gayly we sing, etc.

3 *pp* Faintly, faintly sounds the distant fall;
   Lightly, lightly, woodland echoes call;
   And in their voice we deem we hear
   The tones of friends once gay and dear.
f Pealing, pealing, join the laugh and shout,
      While gayly we sing, etc.

STUDENT'S SONG.

1. A - wake the song of mer - ry greet - ing, Sing
   The notes in - spir - ing, joy re - peat - ing, Sing
   Tra la la la la la la.
   Tra la la la la la la. Let mirth to wis - dom trib - ute pay, But yet be mer - ry when we may. Sing Tra la la la la la la, Sing tra la la la la la la, Sing Tra la la la la la la.

2 'Tis well for thought to find a season,   Sing tra la, etc.
   For study always there's no reason,   Sing tra la, etc.
   We gather knowledge from the past,
   To make life happy while it last.   Sing Tra la, etc.

[*Concluding stanzas on opposite page.*]

LAUGHING AND SINGING.

BRISKLY, WITH LIGHT VOICE.

1. Laugh - ing and sing - ing, Dan - cing and spring - ing,
2. Ev - er be striv - ing, Use - ful - ly liv - ing,
3. While on earth dwell - ing, Ban - ish each feel - ing,

Mer - ri - ly laugh now,—Yes, laugh while you may.
All that is good and is no - ble to learn.
Lur - ing the soul from the path of the wise.

Tä fä Tä fä Tě fě

Shroud-ed in sor - row, Dawn-eth .to - mor - row;
Sea - sons are fly - ing, Man - y are dy - ing,
Laugh-ing and sing - ing, Dan -cing and spring - ing,

Then let the mo - ments pass gai - ly to - day.
Vir - tue's flame bright - ly, then, ev - er should burn.
Now let all voic - es in glad - ness a - rise.

[Concluded from opposite page.]

3 And if the day we give to labor, Sing tra la, etc.
   The evening's due to friend and neighbor,   Sing tra la, etc.
   When nature needful rest designed,
   To strengthen body and the mind.   Sing tra la, ete.

4 Tho' care will come and tribulation,   Sing tra la, etc.
   We 'll sigh not in th' anticipation;   Sing tra la, etc.
   For joy will soon each grief dispel
   From hearts where love and friendship dwell.   Sing tra la, etc.

AUTUMN.

NOT TOO FAST.

1. A no - ble friend good Au - tumn is; He comes, his treas-ures
2. A no - ble friend old Au - tumn is; He comes, his treas-ures

bring - ing; To tempt the taste, and please the sight, His silk - en
bring - ing; To tempt the taste, and please the sight, His silk - en

fringe he's spin-ning; Rich fruit he scat - ters from his wings, And
fringe he's spin-ning; Old Win - ter, call up all your pow'rs, The

if thou dost not choose them, Blame not the boun - teous
snow and whirl - wind mus - ter; We trim the fire and

friend who brings, But him who will not use them.
close the doors, And care not how you blus - ter.

OUR FATHER-LAND.

TUNE,— "Autumn."

Come, one and all, around me stand ;　Old ocean bore from Mammon's marts,
　Come join in swelling chorus;　　　　The plant of freedom hither ;
And praise our goodly native land,　　It blossoms yet, and glads our hearts,
　Our father-land that bore us.　　　　And we'll not let it wither.

THE NEW-YEAR SONG.

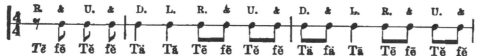

Tĕ fĕ Tĕ fĕ Tă Tă Tĕ fĕ Tĕ fĕ Tă fă Tă Tĕ fĕ Tĕ fĕ

Tä-ä fä Tĕ fĕ Tĕ Tä-ä

1. New-year is come; that he should find us The
2. The stern old year! I'm glad he's 'part - ed! And

same old song, we mourn; But all our faults we
yet I lov'd him well; He brought the best, while

leave be - hind us, With the year that now is gone.
we, weak-heart - ed, Read wrong - ly what be - fell.

3 He loved us: though he brought us sorrow,
 He always taught in love;
 We left the lesson till the morrow,
 And so did not improve.

4 Now thou art come, with smiles so pleasant!
 But say, canst thou do this,—
 Bring back our earliest new year's present,
 The days of childhood bliss.

5 Who sends thee, doubtless, sends thee giving
 As good as we can crave;
 Young year, we hope we may be living
 To bear thee to thy grave.

ALL YONDER IN THE MEADOW.

VEAZIE.

Moderately.

1. All yon-der in the mead-ow Is sun-shine, clear and
2. All yon-der in the moun-tain Is act-ive life and

bright; All yon-der in the sha-dow Is cool-ness and de-
health; All yon-der in the val-ley Is rest and peace-ful

slower.

light, Is cool-ness and de-light.
wealth, Is rest and peace-ful wealth.

3 All brightly in the heavens,
　　The stars at even glow;
　All lovely bloom the flowers,
　‖: The stars of earth, below. :‖

4 Than health, or wealth, or flowers,
　　Than stars or sunshine bright,
　More sweet, more blest, more lovely,
　‖: When heart and heart unite. :‖

PART IV.—TEST-EXERCISES.

It is recommended that before taking up the following test-exercises the pupils go through the first twelve charts, of the New Second Series, and the first eighteen pages of the New Second Music Reader, according to directions on page 3.

These test-exercises are designed to be used as follows:—

First, the teacher writes the exercises upon the blackboard.

Second, calls for volunteers who think they can sing the exercise all alone. Perhaps twelve will indicate their willingness to do their best.

Third, the volunteers are numbered, 1, 2, 3, etc.

Fourth, each pupil is to sing the exercise through, as follows: Number One commences at *a.* When One has sung the first four measures, and commences at *b,* Number Two commences at *a,* when they will be singing together. When Number Two commences at *b;* Number Three begins at *a;* and so on.

If any fail to commence at the right time, or be thrown out of tune, this should be regarded as a break in the chain, and the defective link should be cast aside.

This being in the spirit of a game, it will excite a good deal of interest in the whole class, so that on a second and third trial others will volunteer, and those who failed will like to try again. In schools where twenty minutes' time each day is devoted to music, it would be well to give one lesson each week to this or some other exercise which would test the progress of the pupils individually.

The pupils should beat the time, and, after a clear explanation by the teacher as to how the exercises are to be performed (the key and rate of time being given), should be left entirely alone. It will be better for the teacher to be out of sight of the pupils, during the performance of these exercises, which should never be sung otherwise than as explained above.

The following exercises are by Dr. Lowell Mason.

The following exercises, for testing the ability of the class as to their independence in reading music, are in some respects more simple than those in the form of rounds. Teachers can take their choice between the two. As these exercises are much longer than the rounds, they are to be sung from the books, the pupils beating the time, and proceeded with as follows:—

Take as many pupils as there are phrases in the exercise; have one at a time sing only one phrase, and continue in order, with the melody unbroken. If a pupil fail, let his or her place be taken by another (volunteer), and begin again *with a new exercise,*—that in which the failure occurred being regarded as unfit for further test work till another lesson.

Tä-a fä Tē Tä Tä Tē Tä-a-ē Tä-a Tē

Tē Tä-a fä Tē Tä-a Tē

Tä fä   Tä fä   Tē fē   Tä   Tä   Tē

APPENDIX—TIME-NAMES

The object of this System of Time-Names is to designate the position of each note in a measure of whatever kind of time.

It does not pretend to teach or develop time, but simply to *name* the notes in any given measure. It differs entirely from the Chévré System of Time-Names (which has been adopted in the Tonic-Sol-Fa method in a modified form); as, in this system, the *measure* is the unit, but in the Chévré System the unit is a *"pulse"* or beat.

APPENDIX.

TEACHING TIME WITH THE ADDITION OF THE TIME-NAMES.

CHAPTER I.

SECTION I. — *Double or Two-Part Measure.*

First. The pupils are to be taught double time in the ordinary manner, with the names of the beats (Down and Up), accenting the down beat.

Second. While beating time, the pupils, instead of saying *Down-beat*, are to say Tä (*a* as in fäther); and instead of saying *Up-beat*, they are to say Tä (*a* as in fäte).

EXAMPLE 1

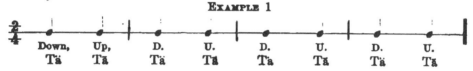

| Down, | Up, | D. | U. | D. | U. | D. | U. |
| Tä | Tä | Tä | Tä | Tä | Tä | Tä | Tä |

Where a sound lasts two beats, the vowel is changed *with* the Up-beat; as in

EXAMPLE 2.

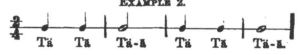

Tä   Tä   Tä-ä   Tä   Tä   Tä-ä

EXAMPLE 3.

At rests, the names are to be uttered in a soft, distinct whisper.

Tä   Tä   Tä   *Tä*   Tä   Tä   Tä   *Tä.*

EXAMPLE 4.

Commencing with the Up-beat.

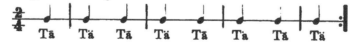

Tä   Tä   Tä   Tä   Tä   Tä   Tä   Tä

SECTION II. — *Triple or Three-Part Measure.*

The beats in Triple Measure are Down, Left, and Up. The Down-beat is accented, and the Left- and Up-beats are unaccented. Some theorists say the Up-beat is slightly accented.

The Time-names are *Tä*, *Tä*, and *Tĕ* (*e* as in mĕ.)

EXAMPLE 5.

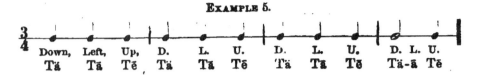

EXAMPLE 6.

Commencing with the Up-beat.

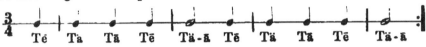

EXAMPLE 7.

Sounds three beats long, in three-four time.

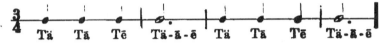

SECTION III. — *Quadruple or Four-Part Measure.*

The beats in quadruple time are Down, Left, Right, and Up. Accented upon the Down and Right beats. The time-names are Tä, Tä, Tē, Tĕ (e as in mĕt).

EXAMPLE 8.

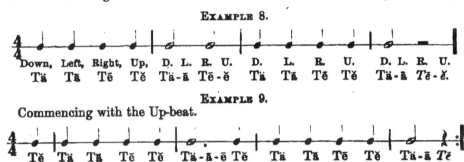

EXAMPLE 9.

Commencing with the Up-beat.

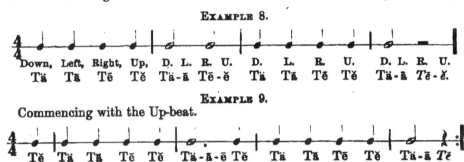

SECTION IV. — *Triple time: Three Eighth-Notes in a Measure.*

EXAMPLE 10.

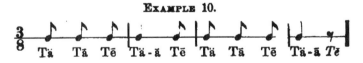

EXAMPLE 11.

Commencing with the Up-beat.

Quadruple Time. — Four Eighth-Notes in a Measure.

EXAMPLE 13.

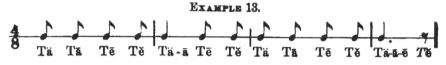

Tä Tă Tē Tĕ Tä-ā Tē Tĕ Tä Tă Tē Tĕ Tä-ā-ē Tĕ

SECTION V.

The other kinds of measures, such as $\frac{6}{4}$ $\frac{6}{8}$ $\frac{9}{8}$ and $\frac{12}{8}$ are to be regarded as two, three or four three-part measures. They are sometimes called *compound measures;* and are to be reduced to the simple measures from which they are derived, and named as simple measures.

Four Three-Four Measures.

EXAMPLE 13.

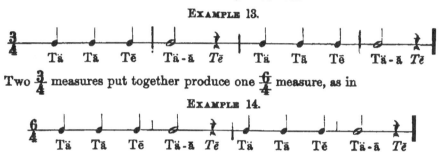

Tä Tă Tē Tä-ā *Tē* Tä Tă Tē Tä-ā *Tē*

Two $\frac{3}{4}$ measures put together produce one $\frac{6}{4}$ measure, as in

EXAMPLE 14.

Tä Tă Tē Tä-ā *Tē* Tä Tă Tē Tä-ā *Tē*

There are three different ways of beating six-part measure: — *First,* Down, Left, Up, twice. *Second,* the first half with the Down-beat, and the second half with the Up-beat. *Third,* with six beats when the time moves slowly, viz. Down, Down, Left; Right, Up, Up.

The second way, that of two beats, is generally the most natural.

Four Measures in Three-Eight Time.

EXAMPLE 15.

Tä Tă Tē Tä-ā Tē Tä Tă Tē Tä-ā Tē.

The above made into Six-Eight Measure.

EXAMPLE 16.

Tä Tă Tē Tä-ā Tē Tä Tă Tē Tä-ā Tē.

Three-Eight Time made into Nine-Eight Time.

EXAMPLE 17.

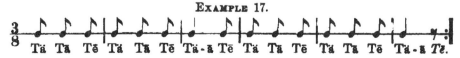

Tä Tă Tē Tä Tă Tē Tä-ā Tē Tä Tă Tē Tä Tă Tē Tä-ā *Tĕ.*

The same in Nine-Eight Time.

EXAMPLE 18.

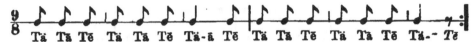

Tä Tä Tĕ Tä Tä Tĕ Tä-ä Tĕ Tä Tä Tĕ Tä Tä Tĕ Tä.- Tĕ

There are two ways of beating the time in $\frac{9}{8}$ measure: — *First*, Down, Left, Up, three times. *Second*, with three beats, Down, Left, and Up. (Three eighth-notes to each beat.)

If the laws of accent be developed carefully, so the pupils understand them perfectly in Double and Triple time, they will spontaneously manifest them selves in all the varieties of compound time, and in all the subdivisions of measures: if they are treated practically, and not talked about too much.

CHAPTER II.

Two Sounds of Equal Length in Each Part of the Measure.

SECTION I. — *Two-Part Time.*

When there are two sounds of equal length in each part of the measure, in two-part time, the time-names are, Tä, fä, Tä, fä.

EXAMPLE 19.

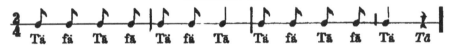

Tä fä Tä fä Tä fä Tä Tä fä Tä fä Tä Tä

EXAMPLE 20.

Commencing after the Up-beat, or on fä

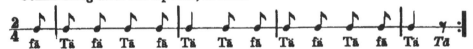

fä Tä fä Tä fä Tä Tä fä Tä fä Tä fä Tä Tä

Lead the pupils to observe that, in examples 19 and 20, Tä and Tä come *with* the beats, and that fä and fä come *after* the beats.

The Dotted Quarter-Note.

EXAMPLE 21.

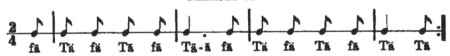

fä Tä fä Tä fä Tä-ä fä Tä fä Tä fä Tä Tä

Lead the pupils to see, in this example, that the dotted quarter-note is sounded during the two beats. That the eighth-note after the dotted quarter is sounded *after* the Up-beat.

SECTION II.— *Triple Time.*

EXAMPLE 22.

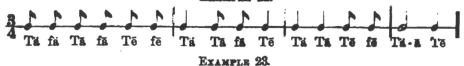

Tä fä Tä fä Tē fē Tä Tä fä Tē Tä Tä Tē fē Tä-ä Tē

EXAMPLE 23.

Commencing with the Up-beat, or Tē, fē.

Tē fē Tä-ä fä Tē fē Tä-ä Tē fē Tä Tä fä Tē fē Tä-ä

To commence promptly, the pupils must have the first two notes in mind, so as to begin *with* the Up-beat.

EXAMPLE 24.

Commencing after the Left-beat, or with fä, Tē, fē.

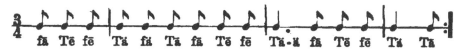

fä Tē fē Tä fä Tä fä Tē fē Tä-ä fä Tē fē Tä Tä

SECTION III.— *Quadruple, or Four-Part Measure.*

EXAMPLE 25.

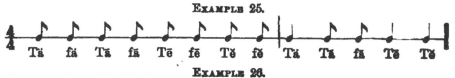

Tä fä Tä fä Tē fē Tē fē Tä Tä fä Tē Tē

EXAMPLE 26.

Commencing with Tē, fē.

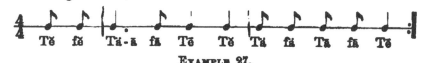

Tē fē Tä-ä fä Tē Tē Tä fä Tä fä Tē

EXAMPLE 27.

Commencing after the Up-beat, or on fē.

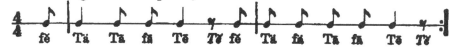

fē Tä Tä fä Tē Tē fē Tä fä Tä fä Tē Tē

CHAPTER III.

SECTION I.— *Four Sounds of Equal Length in Each Part of the Measure.*

Double Time.

When there are four sounds of equal length in each part of the measure in Double Time, they are named, Tä, sä, fä, nä, Tä, zä, fä, nä.

EXAMPLE 28.

Tä zä fä nä Tä zä fä nä   Tä fä nä Tä

Dotted Eighth-Notes.

EXAMPLE 29.

Tä-ä-ä nä Tä fä   Tä fä   Tä   Tä-ä-ä nä Tä fä   Tä   Tä

Triple Time.

EXAMPLE 30.

Tä zä fä nä Tä zä fä nä Tĕ zĕ fĕ nĕ   Tä   Tä fä Tĕ

EXAMPLE 31.

Tä-ä-ä nä Tä zä fä nä Tĕ   Tä fä Tä fä Tĕ fĕ Tä-ä-ä nä Tä   Tĕ

Quadruple time.

EXAMPLE 32.

Tä zä fä nä Tä zä fä nä Tĕ zĕ fĕ nĕ   Tĕ zĕ fĕ nĕ   Tä   Tä fä Tĕ   Tĕ

EXAMPLE 33.

Tä-ä-ä nä Tä-ä-ä nä Tĕ   fĕ Tĕ fĕ Tä-ä-ä nä Tä-ä-ä nä Tĕ   Tĕ

CHAPTER IV.

SECTION I.—*Triplets: Three Sounds of Equal Length in Each Part of the Measure.*

Triplets are usually marked with a figure 3 over or under them, thus:—

When there are three sounds of equal length in each part of a measure, in Double Time, they are named, Tä, rä, lä, Tä, rä, lä.

EXAMPLE 34.

Tä rä lä Tä rä lä Tä rä lä Tä

Triple Time.

EXAMPLE 35.

Quadruple Time.

EXAMPLE 36.

SECTION II.—*Sextolets, or Subdivisions of Triplets.*

The triplet is rarely subdivided. In this respect it differs from compound time. It is sometimes found subdivided in the more difficult forms of rhythm. Below are the Time-Names of one subdivision of triplets, in which there are six sounds of equal length to each beat.

EXAMPLE 37.

Farther subdivisons of triplets are exceptional, and quite outside of rhythmical feeling. This is as far as we deem it necessary to provide time-names in popular music.